Spanish Phrase Book

Spanish translation by
Angela Bailie

Spanish Phrase Book

Edmund Swinglehurst

NEWNES·BOOKS

NEWNES·BOOKS

First published in 1979 by
The Hamlyn Publishing Group Limited
Published in 1983 by Newnes Books,
84–88, The Centre, Feltham, Middlesex, England

© Copyright The Hamlyn Publishing Group Limited 1979
and Newnes Books, a division of
The Hamlyn Publishing Group Limited, 1983

Eighth Impression 1985

ISBN 0 600 38245 1

Printed in Great Britain by
Hazell Watson & Viney Limited,
Member of the BPCC Group,
Aylesbury, Bucks

Distributed in the U.S. by
Larousse & Co. Inc., 572 Fifth Avenue, New York,
New York 10036

Contents

Introduction

The Newnes Spanish Phrase Book is designed to help the reader who has no previous knowledge of the language. With its aid he should be able to make himself readily understood on all occasions and to cope with the host of minor problems – and some major ones – that can arise when on holiday or travelling in Spain.

The key to successful speech in a foreign language is pronunciation, and an outline of the principles of vowel and consonant sounds and their usage in Spanish is to be found at the beginning of this book. This is followed by a section dealing with the essential elements of Spanish grammar. A close study of these two sections and constant reference to them will be of the utmost value: with the pattern of sentence construction in mind and a feeling for the sound of the language, the reader will be well equipped to use the phrases in this book.

These are set out in logical order, beginning with the various means of travel and entry to the country. The section on accommodation covers the whole range from hotels and private houses and villas to youth hostels and camping sites. Particular attention is paid in the chapter on food and drink to the speciality dishes from the different regions and in the section on sport there is a chapter describing the principles of the bullfight. Shopping, too, is covered in detail: whether the reader wishes to take back a souvenir of Spanish leatherwork or fine lace, or to equip his self-catering apartment with a week's supply of groceries, he will find a selection of appropriate phrases easy to refer to and simple to use.

Entertainment, sightseeing, public services, and general conversations in the hotel bar are all covered, and there is an important section of commercial and banking phrases of particular value to the businessman. In addition to carefully chosen phrases, each section includes an appropriate vocabulary which is as comprehensive as possible, and at the end of the book there are quick-reference metric conversion tables for the more important temperatures, weights and measures.

The Newnes Spanish Phrase Book will not only enable the traveller to handle any situation with confidence but will help to make his stay in Spain a more enjoyable one.

Guide to Spanish Pronunciation

This is intended for people with no previous knowledge of Spanish and is based on English pronunciation. This means that it is not entirely accurate but the reader who pays careful attention to this section should, with practice, be able to make himself understood reasonably well in Spanish.

The Vowels

LETTER	APPROXIMATE PRONUNCIATION	EXAMPLE
a	like *a* in father	**patata**
e	like *e* in set	**mesa**
i	1 like *ee* in meet	**chico**
	2 before another vowel like *y* in yet	**tienda**
o	like *o* in hot	**todo**
u	1 like *oo* in shoot	**mucho**
	2 before another vowel like *w* in wet	**bueno**
y	only pronounced as a vowel when alone or at the end of a word, like *ee* in bee	**y, rey**

The Consonants

LETTER	APPROXIMATE PRONUNCIATION	EXAMPLE
d f k l m n p t y	pronounced as in English	
b	1 usually like *b* in back	**barato**
	2 between two vowels has a sound between *b* and *v*	**debido**
c	1 before *e* and *i* like *th* in thick	**centro, cinco**
	2 elsewhere like *c* in cat	**poco**
ch	like *ch* in church	**muchacho**
g	1 before *e* and *i* like *ch* in loch	**gente, surgir**
	2 elsewhere like *g* in go	**gato**
h	always silent in Spanish	**haber**
j	like *ch* in loch	**bajo**
ll	like *lli* in million	**llamar**
ñ	like *ni* in onion	**señor**
qu	like *c* in cat	**que**
r	slightly trilled like the Scottish *r*	**rey**
rr	strongly trilled	**perro**
s	always like *s* in set; never hard, as in rose	**siempre, casa**
v	1 usually like *b* in boy	**vaso**
	2 between two vowels has a sound between *b* and *v*	**ave**
z	like *th* in thick	**manzana**

Stress

Words ending in a vowel are stressed on the last syllable but one: **chico, mañana**.

Words ending in a consonant, except for *n* or *s*, are stressed on the last syllable: **señor, ciudad, hablar**.

Exceptions to these rules have an accent written on the stressed syllable: **aquí, lección, difícil**.

A Little Grammar in Action

Nouns

All nouns in Spanish are either masculine or feminine whether they refer to living beings or inanimate objects. Nouns ending in *-o* are masculine and those ending in *-a* are usually feminine. Nouns ending in a consonant or *-e* may be either masculine or feminine.

Before masculine nouns the word for 'the' (or definite article) is **el** and before feminine nouns it is **la**.

el chico the boy
el hombre the man
la madre the mother
la casa the house
la mujer the woman

To form the plural nouns ending in a vowel add *-s* and those ending in a consonant add *-es*. The word for 'the' is **los** before masculine and **las** before feminine nouns.

los chicos the boys
las mujeres the women

The word for 'a' (or indefinite article) is **un** before a masculine noun and **una** before a feminine noun.

un tren a train
una peseta a peseta

The word 'of' showing possession is translated by **de** in Spanish, **de** and **el** being shortened to **del**.

el libro del chico the boy's book
la madre de la mujer the woman's mother
las puertas de las casas the doors of the houses

4

Adjectives

Adjectives agree in number and gender with the noun they accompany, that is, they change their endings according to whether the noun is masculine, feminine or plural. They generally follow the noun. Adjectives ending in -*o* change to -*a* in the feminine.

el chico pequeño the little boy
la casa roja the red house

Adjectives ending in -*e* and most of those ending in a consonant do not change in the feminine.

el libro azul the blue book
la puerta azul the blue door
un hombre inteligente a clever man
una mujer inteligente a clever woman

To form the plural adjectives ending in -*o*, -*a* or -*e* add -*s*; adjectives ending in a consonant add -*es*.

las chicas bonitas the pretty girls
los libros azules the blue books

To form the comparative and superlative forms put **más** before the adjective.

un libro caro an expensive book
un libro más caro a more expensive book
el libro más caro the most expensive book

Demonstrative Adjectives

The words for 'this' and 'that' are as follows.

este hombre this man
estos hombres these men

esta mujer this woman
estas mujeres these women

Grammar

aquel libro that book
aquellos libros those books

aquella casa that house
aquellas casas those houses

Possessive Adjectives

The words for 'my', 'your', 'his', etc., change their form
according to whether the noun they refer to is masculine,
feminine or plural.

	SINGULAR	PLURAL
my	**mi**	**mis**
your	**tu**	**tus**
his/her/its	**su**	**sus**
our	**nuestro(a)**	**nuestros(as)**
your	**vuestro(a)**	**vuestros(as)**
their	**su**	**sus**

mi hijo my son
mis padres my parents

tu hermana your sister
tus amigos your friends

su madre his/her mother
sus libros his/her books

nuestro coche our car
nuestras cartas our letters

vuestra casa your house
vuestros lápices your pencils

su maleta their suitcase
sus cuartos their rooms

Personal Pronouns

The words for 'I', 'you', 'he', etc., are as follows.

1 When used as the subject of a verb:

yo canto	I sing
tu cantas	you sing
usted canta (pol. form)	you sing
el canta	he sings
ella canta	she sings
nosotros(as) cantamos	we sing
vosotros(as) cantáis	you sing
ustedes cantan (pol. form)	you sing
ellos(as) cantan	they sing

2 When used as the direct object of a verb:

Señor López me conoce	Señor López knows me
te	you
le (pol. form)	you (masc.)
la (pol. form)	you (fem.)
le/lo	him
la	her
nos	us
os	you
los (pol. form)	you (masc.)
las (pol. form)	you (fem.)
los/les	them (masc.)
las	them (fem.)

3 When used as the indirect object of a verb:

Señor López me dice	Señor López says to me
te	you
le (pol. form)	you
le	him
le	her
nos	us
os	you
les (pol. form)	you
les	them

When used as the direct or indirect object pronouns are placed in front of the verb. When two pronouns in the third person occur together the indirect pronoun **le** or **les** is replaced by **se**.

Señor López se lo dice	Señor López tells it to him

4 When used after a preposition:

Estos libros son para mí	These books are for me
ti	you
usted (pol. form)	you
el	him
ella	her
nosotros(as)	us
vosotros(as)	you
ustedes (pol. form)	you
ellos	them (masc.)
ellas	them (fem.)

In Spanish the polite way of addressing people is to use **usted** (often abbreviated to **Vd**) and **le** when talking to one person, and **ustedes** (often abbreviated to **Vds**) and **les** when talking to more than one person. **Tu**, etc., and its plural **vosotros** are the familiar forms and should be used only when speaking to children, relations and close friends.

Verbs

The whole subject of Spanish verbs is too complicated for
detailed discussion in a phrase book but for the traveller who
wants a quick grasp of verbs with which he can communicate
while staying in Spain the following basic rules will be useful.

Regular Verbs

Most Spanish verbs are regular in their formation and fall
into one of three categories or conjugations. Note that the
subject pronouns are usually omitted (except for the polite
forms **usted** and **ustedes**) since the verb endings show
which person is referred to.

1 Verbs ending in *-ar* in
the infinitive.

2 Verbs ending in *-er* in
the infinitive.

comprar	to buy	vender	to sell
yo compro	I buy	**yo vendo**	I sell
tu compras	you buy	**tu vendes**	you sell
usted compra	you buy	**usted vende**	you sell
él compra	he buys	**él vende**	he sells
/ella	/she	**/ella**	/she
nosotros compramos	we buy	**nosotros vendemos**	we sell
vosotros compráis	you buy	**vosotros vendéis**	you sell
ustedes compran	you buy	**ustedes venden**	you sell
ellos compran	they buy	**ellos venden**	they sell
/ellas		**/ellas**	

3 Verbs ending in *-ir* in the infinitive.

vivir	to live
yo vivo	I live
tu vives	you live
usted vive	you live
él vive	he lives
/ella	/she
nosotros vivimos	we live
vosotros vivís	you live
ustedes viven	you live
ellos viven	they live
/ellas	

To form the negative of a verb **no** is placed before it:

No vendemos libros we don't sell books

Irregular Verbs

The following are a few of the more useful common irregular verbs.

ser	to be	estar	to be
yo soy	I am	yo estoy	I am
tu eres	you are	tu estás	you are
usted es	you are	usted está	you are
él es	he is	él está	he is
/ella	/she	/ella	/she
nosotros somos	we are	nosotros estamos	we are
vosotros sois	you are	vosotros estáis	you are
ustedes son	you are	ustedes están	you are
ellos son	they are	ellos están	they are
/ellas		/ellas	

'To be' is translated by **ser** when it describes a permanent condition. It is translated by **estar** when it indicates a temporary state or location.

el hielo es frío ice is cold
es español he is Spanish
estamos en Inglaterra we are in England

haber	to have	tener	to have, possess
yo he	I have	**yo tengo**	I have
tu has	you have	**tu tienes**	you have
usted ha	you have	**usted tiene**	you have
él ha	he has	**él tiene**	he has
/ella	/she	/ella	/she
nosotros habemos	we have	**nosotros tenemos**	we have
vosotros habéis	you have	**vosotros tenéis**	you have
ustedes han	you have	**ustedes tienen**	you have
ellos han	they have	**ellos tienen**	they have
/ellas		/ellas	

haber is used only to form the compound tenses of verbs :

he comprado un lápiz I have bought a pencil

tener is used in all the other meanings of 'have'.

tengo un lápiz I have a pencil

dar	to give	decir	to say
yo doy	I give	**yo digo**	I say
tu das	you give	**tu dices**	you say
usted da	you give	**usted dice**	you say
él da	he gives	**él dice**	he says
/ella	/she	/ella	/she
nosotros damos	we give	**nosotros decimos**	we say
vosotros dáis	you give	**vosotros decís**	you say
ustedes dan	you give	**ustedes dicen**	you say
ellos dan	they give	**ellos dicen**	they say
/ellas		/ellas	

Grammar

hacer	to make, do	**ir**	to go
yo hago	I make	**yo voy**	I go
tu haces	you make	**tu vas**	you go
usted hace	you make	**usted va**	you go
él hace	he makes	**él va**	he goes
/ella	/she	**/ella**	/she
nosotros hacemos	we make	**nosotros vamos**	we go
vosotros hacéis	you make	**vosotros váis**	you go
ustedes hacen	you make	**ustedes van**	you go
ellos hacen	they make	**ellos van**	they go
/ellas		**/ellas**	

poder	to be able, can	**poner**	to put
yo puedo	I can	**yo pongo**	I put
tu puedes	you can	**tu pones**	you put
usted puede	you can	**usted pone**	you put
él puede	he can	**él pone**	he puts
/ella	/she	**/ella**	/she
nosotros podemos	we can	**nosotros ponemos**	we put
vosotros podéis	you can	**vosotros ponéis**	you put
ustedes pueden	you can	**ustedes ponen**	you put
ellos pueden	they can	**ellos ponen**	they put
/ellas		**/ellas**	

querer	to want	**traer**	to bring
yo quiero	I want	**yo traigo**	I bring
tu quieres	you want	**tu traes**	you bring
usted quiere	you want	**usted trae**	you bring
él quiere	he wants	**él trae**	he brings
/ella	/she	**/ella**	/she
nosotros queremos	we want	**nosotros traemos**	we bring
vosotros queréis	you want	**vosotros traéis**	you bring
ustedes quieren	you want	**ustedes traen**	you bring
ellos quieren	they want	**ellos traen**	they bring
/ellas		**/ellas**	

venir	to come	**ver**	to see
yo vengo	I come	**yo veo**	I see
tu vienes	you come	**tu ves**	you see
usted viene	you come	**usted ve**	you see
él viene	he comes	**él ve**	he sees
/ella	/she	**/ella**	/she
nosotros venimos	we come	**nosotros vemos**	we see
vosotros venís	you come	**vosotros véis**	you see
ellos vienen	they come	**ellos ven**	they see
/ellas		**/ellas**	

Spanish Spoken

The Spanish-speaking world is a large one comprising not only Spain and its islands, which include the Balearics and the Canaries, but the whole of the Latin American continent except Brazil and, perhaps surprisingly to those who do not know the history of Imperial Spain, the Philippines.

Spain

The regions of Spain most well known to the visitor are Castile, the Basque country, Catalonia, Andalusia and the Mediterranean coast. In each of them is an important city that epitomises the character of the region that surrounds it.

MADRID, in the centre of Spain, is the seat of government and a fine city which has accumulated the wealth of the Spanish Empire. Here amid the sophisticated life of a capital city are fine buildings and boulevards, the famous Prado gallery, a fascinating old town, and a palace. Nearby are the Escorial Palace and Monastery to the north, and Toledo to the south.

SAN SEBASTIAN is an important resort and summer residence of the government. A gateway to the Cantabrian mountains and the caves of Altamira with their prehistoric paintings, the resort is also a gastronomic centre.

BARCELONA, capital of Catalonia, is a large port with an old city full of picturesque narrow streets. A cathedral, an art gallery containing Picasso's early work, a medieval museum, and a model town 'Pueblo Español' containing examples of the architecture of all Spain are the main features.

SEVILLE is the heart of Andalusia and its architecture reflects the mixture of Spanish and Moorish cultures which combine to enrich southern Spain. There is a fine cathedral, the Alcázar palace, museums, bars and restaurants where flamenco is played and danced. To the west of Andalusia lies Granada, with its gardens and its own famous Moorish palace, the 'Alhambra'.

VALENCIA is the third city of Spain and a huge port. In the old quarter is the cathedral and a fifteenth-century palace. The countryside around abounds with fruit orchards, and the famous resorts of the Costa Blanca and the Costa del Azahar lie along the coast.

THE SPANISH ISLANDS of the Balearic archipelago are popular holiday regions, especially in summer, while the Canary Islands in the Atlantic also attract a winter clientele because of their mild climate. The islands of this group are surprisingly varied and landscapes range from tropical banana-covered valleys to bare volcanic mountains.

Wherever you travel in these regions you will find that a few words spoken in Spanish will help to establish a friendly atmosphere. Here are some simple phrases of greeting and leave-taking:

Good morning.	**Buenos días.**
Good afternoon.	**Buenas tardes.**
Good evening.	**Buenas tardes/noches.**
Good night.	**Buenas noches.**
How are you?	**¿Cómo está usted?**
I'm very pleased to meet you.	**Tanto gusto.**
How do you do?	**Encantado de conocerle.**
Goodbye.	**Adiós.**

Some words of courtesy:

Please.	**Por favor.**
Thank you.	**Gracias.**
It's very kind of you.	**Es usted muy amable.**
You are welcome.	**De nada.**
Not at all.	**No hay de qué.**

And some questions:

Where is the hotel?	**¿Dónde está el Hotel?**
What did you say?	**¿Qué dijo?**
When does the train leave?	**¿Cuándo sale el tren?**
Who are you?	**¿Quién es usted?**
How much does it cost?	**¿Cuánto cuesta?**
Which is the road to ...?	**¿Cuál es la carretera a ...?**
Why are we waiting?	**¿Por qué estamos esperando?**

Finally some useful common phrases:

Yes.	**Sí.**
No.	**No.**
Why?	**¿Por qué?**
How?	**¿Cómo?**
When?	**¿Cuándo?**
What?	**¿Qué?**
Where?	**¿Dónde?**
How much?	**¿Cuánto?**

How many?	**¿Cuántos?**
Please speak slowly.	**Hable despacio por favor.**
I do not understand Spanish very well.	**No entiendo muy bien el español.**
Will you write it down please?	**¿Lo puede escribir por favor?**
How do I say ...?	**¿Cómo se dice ...?**
What is the meaning of ...?	**¿Qué significa ...?**
Please show me how this works.	**Enséñeme cómo funciona por favor.**
How far is it to ...?	**¿Cuál es la distancia a ...?**
Where is the nearest ...?	**¿Cuál es el próximo ...?**
What time is it?	**¿Qué hora es?**
Will you please help me?	**¿Me puede ayudar por favor?**
Can you point to where we are on this map?	**¿Me puede señalar dónde estamos en este mapa?**
Which way do I go?	**¿Cómo voy?**
Is there an official tourist office here?	**¿Hay aquí una Oficina de Turismo?**
Where is the station/bus terminus/bus stop?	**¿Dónde está la estación/terminal de autobús/parada de autobús?**
Where do I buy a ticket?	**¿Dónde puedo comprar un billete?**
Am I too early?	**¿He llegado demasiado temprano?**
It is too late.	**Es demasiado tarde.**

We have missed the train.	Hemos perdido el tren.
Do I turn right/left?	¿Tuerzo a la derecha/izquierda?
Do I go straight ahead?	¿Voy todo a derecho?
What is the name of this street?	¿Cómo se llama esta calle?
How do I get to ...?	¿Cómo voy a ...?
How much does it cost?	¿Cuánto cuesta?
It is too expensive.	Es demasiado caro.
Please give me the change.	Me de el cambio, por favor.
I am tired	Estoy cansado.
I am hungry/thirsty.	Tengo hambre/sed.
It is very hot/cold.	Hace mucho calor/frío.
Please take me to my hotel.	¿Me lleva al hotel por favor?
Is the service included?	¿Está incluído el servicio?
Thank you very much.	Muchas gracias.

And some idiomatic expressions:

Go away.	Váyase.
Leave me alone.	Déjeme en paz.
Shut up.	Cállese.
How goes it?	¿Cómo va?
So so.	Así así.
You're joking.	Usted me toma el pelo.
Don't move.	No se mueva.
That's it.	Eso es.

You're right.	**Lleva razón.**
Carry on.	**Prosiga.**

All Aboard

Journeys through Spain are easy on the main routes, but once
you leave the beaten track, travelling is more difficult –
though never dull – because of the centuries of history that
have left their mark on every town and village. Though air
travel is, of course, the quickest way to get about and internal
airlines provide an excellent service, train and coach or car are
the more rewarding means of transport. Railways are good
and there is some interesting scenery on routes such as
Hendaye on the French border to Madrid, or along the coast
from Barcelona to the south. **Talgo** is a luxury diesel express,
Taf is a diesel express, **Expreso** is a long-distance train with
a few stops, **Rápido** is a fast but stopping train, **Automotor**,
a short-distance diesel train and **Omnibus**, an ordinary train.

The main highways are also well-cared for and there are a few
autoroutes. Service stations are not plentiful, and the level of
petrol in the tank should not be allowed to fall too low. If you
have time, travel slowly; this is how you reach the heart of the
country and where a halting conversation can create a warmth
of communication that remains a long time in the memory.

Arrivals and Departures
Going through Passport Control and Customs

At most of the main gateway airports and ports there will be
someone with a smattering of English, but this is not the case
at all frontier posts. It is useful, therefore, to know one or two
basic phrases. Apart from making communication easier, they
help to establish a friendly relationship with officials and
often smooth the passage through frontiers.

Good morning/afternoon/evening.	**Buenos días/tardes/noches.**
Here is my passport.	**Aquí está mi pasaporte.**
I am on holiday/on business.	**Estoy de vacaciones/de negocios.**
I am visiting relatives/friends.	**Estoy visitando a la familia/los amigos.**
Here is my vaccination certificate.	**Aquí está mi certificado de vacunación.**
The visa is stamped on page X.	**El visado está estampado en la pagina X.**
They did not stamp my passport at the entry port.	**No estamparon mi pasaporte en el puerto de entrada.**
Will you please stamp my passport? It will be a souvenir of my holiday.	**¿Me estampa el pasaporte, por favor? Será un recuerdo de mis vacaciones.**
I will stay a few days/two weeks/a month.	**Permaneceré unos días/dos semanas/un mes.**
I am in transit.	**Estoy de paso.**
My wife and I have a joint passport.	**Mi mujer y yo tenemos un pasaporte común.**
The children are on my wife's passport.	**Los niños están en el pasaporte de mi esposa.**
I didn't realise it had expired.	**No me di cuenta de que había caducado.**
Can I telephone the British consulate?	**¿Puedo llamar al consulado británico?**
I have nothing to declare.	**No tengo nada que declarar.**

Arrivals and Departures

Do you want me to open my cases? Which one?	¿Quiere que abra mis maletas? ¿Cuál?
They are all personal belongings.	Todos son efectos personales.
I have a few small gifts for my friends.	Tengo unos pocos regalos pequeños para mis amigos.
I have 200 cigarettes, some wine and a bottle of spirits.	Tengo doscientos cigarrillos, vino y una botella de licor.
They are for my personal consumption.	Son para mi propia consumición.
Do I have to pay duty?	¿Tengo que pagar derechos de aduana?
I have no other luggage.	No tengo más equipaje.
Do you want to see my handbag/briefcase?	¿Quiere ver mi bolso/cartera?
I can't find my keys.	No puedo encontrar mis llaves.
I have 2000 pesetas in currency, and £100 in travellers' cheques.	Tengo dos mil pesetas en efectivo, y cien libras de cheques de viajero.
I can't afford to pay duty.	No puedo pagar los derechos de aduana.
Can you keep it in bond?	¿Puede guardarlo como depósito bajo fianza?
Here is a list of the souvenirs I have bought.	Aquí tiene una lista de los regalos que he comprado.
You haven't marked my suitcase.	No ha marcado mi maleta.
May I leave now?	¿Me puedo ir ahora?

At Airports, Terminals and Stations

Where can I find a porter?	¿Dónde puedo encontrar un mozo?
a luggage trolley?	una carretilla de equipaje?
the left luggage office?	la consigna?
my registered luggage?	mi equipaje facturado?
Have you seen the representative of my travel company?	¿Ha visto al representante de mi compañía de viajes?
Take my bag to the bus/taxi/car.	Lleve mi bolso al autobús/taxi/coche.
How much per case?	¿Cuánto por maleta?

Toilets

Where is the ladies'/gentlemen's toilet?	¿Dónde está el lavabo de señoras/de caballeros?
Have you any soap?	¿Tiene jabón?
toilet paper?	papel higiénico?
a clean towel?	una toalla limpia?
a comb or hairbrush?	un peine o cepillo de pelo?
Shall I leave a tip?	¿Dejo propina?

Telephone

Where are the public telephones?	¿Dónde están los teléfonos públicos?
I need a telephone directory.	Necesito una guía telefónica.
Where can I get some change?	¿Dónde puedo obtener cambio?

Airports, Terminals and Stations

Can I dial this number or do I ask the operator?	¿Puedo marcar este número o se lo pido a la telefonista?
Hullo.	¿Dígame? (answering) ¡Oiga! (calling).
You need a token.	Necesita una ficha.
May I have Madrid 1234?	¿Me da Madrid doce treinta y cuatro?
Can I reverse the charges?	¿Puede cobrar al número llamado?
I want a person-to-person call.	Quiero una llamada personal.
I have been cut off.	Me han cortado.
You gave me the wrong number.	Me dió el número equivocado.
Is she not in?	¿No está?
Tell her I called. My name is ...	Digalé que he llamado. Mi nombre es ...

Taxi Rank

Where can I get a taxi?	¿Dónde puedo coger un taxi?
Please get me a taxi.	Por favor llame un taxi.
Take me to Puerta del Sol/this address.	Lléveme a la Puerta del Sol/a esta dirección.
How much will it cost?	¿Cuánto costará?
That's too much.	Es demasiado.
Turn right/left at the next corner.	Tuerza a la derecha/ izquierda en la próxima esquina.

Go straight on.	**Vaya todo a derecho.**
I'll tell you when to stop.	**Yo le diré cuando tiene que parar.**
Stop.	**Pare.**
I'm in a hurry.	**Llevo prisa.**
Take it easy.	**Vaya despacio.**
Can you please carry my bags?	**¿Puede llevar mis maletas, por favor?**

Signs

Booking Office	**Despacho de billetes**
Cars Check-in Desk	**Control de coches**
Coach Station	**Estación de autobuses**
Escalator	**Escalera móvil**
Exit	**Salida**
Information Office	**Oficina de Información**
Left Luggage	**Consigna**
Platform	**Andén**
Porters	**Mozos**
Toilet	**Servicios**
Underground	**Metro**
Waiting Room	**Sala de espera**
Bus Stop	**Parada de autobús**

Newsstand/Kiosk

Have you got an English paper or magazine?	¿Tiene un periódico o una revista inglesa?
any paperbacks?	libros en rústica?
Which is the local paper?	¿Cuál es el periódico local?
Do you sell (train) timetables?	¿Tiene horarios (de trenes)?
Do you sell a guide/map to the city?	¿Tiene una guía/un mapa de la ciudad?
Have you any writing paper and envelopes?	¿Tiene papel de escribir y sobres?
a ball point pen?	un bolígrafo?
some string?	cuerda?
sellotape?	cinta adhesiva?
matches?	cerillas?
stamps?	sellos?

Information Bureau

Is there an information burea here?	¿Hay aquí una oficina de información?
Have you any leaflets?	¿Tiene algún folleto?
Have you a guide to the hotels?	¿Tiene un prospecto sobre los hoteles?
pensions?	las pensiones?
youth hostels?	los albergues para jóvenes?
camp sites?	los campings?
Do you find accommodation for visitors?	¿Buscan ustedes alojamiento para los visitantes?

I want a first-class/second-class hotel.	Quiero un hotel de primera clase/segunda clase.
a pension.	una pensión.
a double room.	una habitación doble.
just a single room.	sólo una habitación sencilla.
We'll go right away.	Vamos inmediatamente.
How do I get there?	¿Cómo voy ahí?

At Airports

Where is the check-in desk?	¿Dónde está la oficina de control?
Can I take this in the cabin?	¿Puedo llevar esto a la cabina?
Do I have to pay excess?	¿Tengo que pagar exceso?
You haven't given me a luggage claim tag.	No me ha dado un talón de reclamo para el equipaje.
I've missed my flight. Can you give me another flight?	He perdido mi vuelo. ¿Me puede dar otro?
Is there a bar on the other side of the customs barrier?	¿Hay un bar al otro lado de la barrera de aduanas?
Where is the flight indicator?	¿Dónde está el indicador de vuelos?
Is there a duty-free shop?	¿Hay una tienda libre de derechos de aduana?
Is there another way to go up/ down other than by escalator?	¿Hay otro modo de subir/ bajar aparte de la escalera móvil?
Where can I get some flight insurance?	¿Dónde puedo obtener un seguro de vuelo?

Airports, Terminals and Stations

Is there a wheelchair available?	¿Hay una silla de ruedas disponible?
Is the flight delayed?	¿Ha sido diferido el vuelo?
At what time do we land?	¿A que hora aterrizamos?

At Railway Stations

Where is the ticket office?	¿Dónde está el despacho de billetes?
One first-class/second-class return ticket to Madrid.	Un billete de primera clase/ segunda clase de ida y vuelta a Madrid.
on the express.	en el Expreso.
rapide.	rápido.
direct.	directo.
omnibus.	ómnibus.
autorail.	automotor.
How much is the ticket?	¿Cuánto cuesta el billete?
How much is a child's fare?	¿Cuánto es un billete de niño?
Can I reserve a seat/a couchette/ a sleeping berth?	¿Puedo reservar un asiento/ una litera/un coche-cama?
Is there a supplement to pay?	¿Hay que pagar suplemento?
Do I have to change?	¿Tengo que transbordar?
Will there be a restaurant car on the train?	¿Habrá coche-restaurante en el tren?
Where must I change?	¿Dónde tengo que transbordar?
Where is the platform for the train to Bilbao?	¿Dónde está el andén para el tren a Bilbao?

| Does my friend need a platform ticket? | ¿Necesita mi amigo un billete de andén? |
| What time does the train leave? | ¿A qué hora sale el tren? |

At a Port

Which is quay number six?	¿Cuál es el muelle número seis?
Where is the car ferry terminal?	¿Dónde está la terminal del transbordador?
At what time can I go on board?	¿A qué hora puedo ir a bordo?
Will there be an announcement when visitors must disembark?	¿Habrá un anuncio cuando las visitas deben desembarcar?

VOCABULARY

bench	el banco
bus driver	el conductor
clock	el reloj
exit	la salida
gate	la entrada
guard	el jefe de tren
left luggage office	la consigna
lockers	los casilleros
porter	el mozo
security officer	el oficial de seguridad
station buffet	la cafetería (de estación)
station master	el jefe de estación
tannoy	el altavoz
ticket collector	el revisor
vending machine	el distribuidor automático
waiting room	la sala de espera

En Route

General Expressions

At what time do we start/take off?	**¿A qué hora salimos/despegamos?**
Why is there a delay?	**¿Por qué hay retraso?**
Have I got time to go to the toilet?	**¿Tengo tiempo de ir al wáter?**
I have mislaid my ticket.	**He perdido mi billete.**
Take my address and passport number.	**Tome mi dirección y el número del pasaporte.**
Is this seat reserved?	**¿Está reservado este asiento?**

Travelling by Air

Are you the Chief Steward/Stewardess?	**¿Es usted el Jefe de camareros/la Azafata?**
Which button do I press to call you?	**¿Que botón aprieto para llamarle?**
Can you help me to adjust my seat?	**¿Puede ayudarme a ajustar mi asiento?**
Shall I fasten my seat belt?	**¿Abrocho mi cinturón?**
I haven't got a sick bag.	**No tengo una bolsa de papel.**
How high are we flying?	**¿A qué altitud volamos?**
What speed are we doing?	**¿A qué velocidad vamos?**
What town is that down there?	**¿Qué ciudad es esa de abajo?**
Is there a map of the route?	**¿Hay un mapa de la ruta?**

Are there any duty-free goods available?	**¿Hay artículos libres de impuestos?**
Can I pay you in foreign currency/English money?	**¿Puedo pagar en moneda extranjera/dinero inglés?**
The airvent is stuck.	**El conducto de aire está bloqueado.**
May I change my seat?	**¿Puedo cambiar mi asiento?**

VOCABULARY

aircraft	**el avión**
air terminal	**el aeropuerto**
arrival gate	**la llegada de viajeros**
ashtray	**el cenicero**
flight deck	**la cubierta de vuelo**
fuselage	**el fuselaje**
jet engine	**el reactor**
light	**la luz**
luggage shelf	**el portaequipajes**
propeller	**la hélice**
tail	**la cola**
tray meal	**la comida en bandeja**
window	**la ventanilla**
wing	**el ala**

SIGNS

Fasten your seat belt	**Abrochense los cinturones**
Emergency exit	**Salida de emergencia**
No smoking	**Prohibido fumar**

Travelling

Travelling by Motor Rail

I have booked my car by motor rail to Madrid.	**He hecho una reserva para mi coche en el auto expreso a Madrid.**
Does the ticket include insurance?	**¿Incluye seguro el billete?**
At what time must I report?	**¿A qué hora me debo presentar?**
Where is the loading platform?	**¿Dónde está el andén de carga?**
Shall I lock the car?	**¿Cierro el coche?**
Can I leave my belongings in the car?	**¿Puedo dejar mis cosas en el coche?**
Where is our compartment?	**¿Cuál es nuestro departamento?**
At what time do I have to drive off?	**¿A qué hora tengo que salir (en el coche)?**

Travelling by Rail

Can you tell me where carriage 5 is?	**¿Puede decirme dónde está el vagón número cinco?**
I have a couchette reservation.	**Tengo una reserva de litera.**
This is my seat reservation.	**Esta es mi reserva de asiento.**
Is this seat taken?	**¿Está ocupado este asiento?**
Is the dining car at the front or the back?	**¿Está el coche-restaurante delante o detrás?**
Two tickets for the first service, please.	**Dos billetes para el primer servicio, por favor.**

Is the buffet car open throughout the journey?	¿Está el buffet abierto todo el tiempo?
Can I leave my big case in the baggage car?	¿Puedo dejar mi maleta grande en el vagón de equipajes?
Is there an observation car?	¿Hay un vagón-mirador?
What station is this?	¿Qué estación es esta?
The heating is on/off/too high/too low.	La calefacción está conectada/desconectada/demasiado alta/demasiado baja.
I can't open/close the window.	No puedo abrir/cerrar la ventanilla.
Where do I have to change?	¿Dónde tengo que transbordar?
Is this where I get my connection for Malaga?	¿Es aquí dónde cojo mi combinación para Málaga?

VOCABULARY

blanket	la manta
corridor	el pasillo
compartment	el departamento
cushion	el almohadón
luggage rack	la rejilla
non smoking	prohibido fumar
sleeping berth	la litera
sleeping car	el coche-cama
sliding door	la puerta corrediza

Travelling

Do not lean out of the window	**Es peligroso asomarse al exterior**
Do not use the toilet while the train is stationary	**No utilice el wáter cuando el tren esté parado**

Travelling on a Ship

Where is the purser's office?	**¿Dónde está la oficina del contable?**
Please will you show me to my cabin?	**¿Por favor, me puede llevar a mi cabina?**
Are you the steward?	**¿Es usted el camarero?**
Is there a children's nursery/ a shop/a gymnasium?	**¿Hay un cuarto de los niños/ una tienda/un gimnasio?**
Where can I get some seasick tablets?	**¿Dónde puedo obtener pastillas para el mareo?**
On which side do we disembark?	**¿En qué lado desembarcamos?**
The sea is calm/rough.	**El mar está en calma/bravo.**
What are those birds? Seagulls?	**¿Qué son esos pájaros? ¿Gaviotas?**

VOCABULARY

aft	**la popa**
anchor	**la ancla**
bridge	**el puente**
captain	**el capitán**
crew	**la tripulación**

34

deck	la cubierta
funnel	la chimenea
lifebelt	el cinturón salvavidas
lifeboat	el bote salvavidas
mast	el mástil
officer	el oficial
port (harbour)	el puerto
port (left)	el babor
propeller	la hélice
radar	el radar
raft	la balsa
rail	la barandilla
starboard	el estribor

SIGNS

Danger – Propellers	**Peligro—Hélices**

Travelling by Coach

Is this the coach for Torremolinos?	**¿Es este el autocar a Torremolinos?**
Can I sit near the driver?	**¿Puedo sentarme cerca del conductor?**
Are the seats numbered?	**¿Están los asientos numerados?**
Do I pay on the coach?	**¿Pago dentro del autocar?**
How often does it stop?	**¿Cuántas veces para?**
Would you mind closing the window? It's draughty.	**¿Le importa cerrar la ventanilla? Hay corriente.**
Can you help me with my luggage?	**¿Me puede ayudar con mi equipaje?**

35

Travelling

VOCABULARY

back seat	**el asiento de atrás**
driver	**el conductor**
foot rest	**el apoyapié**
front seat	**el asiento delantero**
guide	**el guía**
luggage compartment	**el compartimiento del equipaje**

Buses and Metro

Where is the bus stop?	**¿Dónde está la parada del autobús?**
Does one have to queue?	**¿Tiene uno que hacer fila?**
Do I need a queue ticket?	**¿Necesito un billete para la fila?**
Can I buy a book of tickets?	**¿Puedo comprar un librillo de billetes?**
Do you go by the Prado?	**¿Pasa usted por el Prado?**
Will you tell me when we reach the Avenida José Antonio?	**¿Me puede avisar cuando lleguemos a la Avenida de José Antonio?**
I want to get off at the next stop.	**Quiero bajar en la próxima parada.**
Will you ring the bell please?	**¿Puede tocar el timbre por favor?**
I want to go to the Plaza de España.	**Quiero ir a la Plaza de España.**
Which line do I take?	**¿Qué linea tomo?**
Do I have to change?	**¿Tengo que cambiar?**

At what time is the last metro?	¿A qué hora es el último metro?
Here is a metro map.	Aquí tiene un mapa del metro.

VOCABULARY

automatic doors	las puertas automáticas
barrier	la barrera
escalator	la escalera móvil

SIGNS

Reserved for war wounded	Reservado para los mutilados de guerra

Other Vehicles

Where can I hire a bicycle?	¿Dónde puedo alquilar una bicicleta?
a moped?	un ciclomotor?
a tricycle?	un triciclo?
a tandem?	un tandem?
Please put some air in this tyre.	Por favor, infle este neumático.
One of the spokes is broken.	Uno de los radios está roto.
The brake is not working.	El freno no funciona.
Do you have a bicycle with gears?	¿Tiene una bicicleta con marchas?
The saddle needs lowering/raising.	El sillín necesita bajar/subir.

37

Travelling

Are there any horse-drawn vehicles at this resort?	¿Hay algún vehículo tirado por caballos en este lugar?
Will you put the roof down please?	¿Puede bajar la capota, por favor?
Can the children sit with the driver?	¿Pueden los niños sentarse con el conductor?
Are the cable cars working?	¿Funciona el teleférico?
Is there a chairlift?	¿Hay telesilla?
Please adjust the safety bar for me.	Por favor ajuste la barra de seguridad por mí.
Do they run frequently?	¿Funcionan muy a menudo?
How high is the upper station?	¿A qué altitud está la estación de arriba?
Can I walk down?	¿Puedo bajar andando?
Do you sell season tickets?	¿Vende billetes de temporada?

VOCABULARY

bicycle pump	la bomba de bicicleta
carrier	el portaequipajes
chain	la cadena
donkey	el burro
handlebar	el manillar
harness	las guarniciones
lamp (of car, etc.)	el faro
mudguard	el guardabarros
pedal	el pedal
rear light	la luz trasera
ski-lift	el telesquí
skis	los esquíes

sledge	**el trineo**
toboggan	**el tobogán**
whip	**el látigo**

Walking About

IN TOWN

Is this the main shopping street?	**¿Es esta la calle principal?**
Where is the town hall/police station?	**¿Dónde está el ayuntamiento/comisaría?**
Can you direct me to the tourist office?	**¿Podría indicarme dónde está la oficina turística?**
In what part of town are the theatres/nightclubs?	**¿En qué parte de la ciudad están los teatros/clubs de noche?**
Can I get there by bus/underground/on foot?	**¿Puedo ir allí en autobús/metro/a pie?**
Where is the nearest station/bus stop/taxi rank?	**¿Dónde está la estación más cercana/parada de autobús/parada de taxis?**
Is there a market in the town?	**¿Hay un mercado en la ciudad?**
What day is market day?	**¿Que día hay mercado?**
Is the business centre near?	**¿Está cerca el centro comercial?**
Must one cross at the traffic lights?	**¿Debe uno cruzar en las luces de tráfico?**
Do pedestrians have right of way here?	**¿Tienen los peatones derecho de paso aquí?**
Is there a public toilet near?	**¿Hay un wáter cercano?**

Travelling

VOCABULARY

castle	el castillo
cathedral	la catedral
cemetry	el cementerio
church	la iglesia
city centre	el centro urbano
concert hall	la sala de conciertos
courts	el juzgado
docks	los muelles
exhibition	la exposición
factory	la fábrica
fortress	la fortaleza
fountain	la fuente
government buildings	la casa del gobierno
gardens	los jardines
harbour	el puerto
lake	el lago
monastery	el monasterio
monument	el monumento
museum	el museo
old town	la ciudad vieja
opera house	el teátro de la ópera
palace	el palacio
park	el parque
ruins	las ruinas
shopping centre	el centro comercial
stadium	el estadio
statue	la estatua
stock exchange	la bolsa
subway	el pasaje subterráneo
traffic lights	las luces de tráfico
tower	la torre
university	la universidad
zoo	el zoo

IN THE COUNTRY

May I walk through here?	¿Puedo pasar por aquí?
Is this a public footpath?	¿Es esta una senda pública?
Do I need permission to fish?	¿Necesito permiso para pescar?
Which way is north/south/east/west?	¿Qué ruta es norte/sur/este/oeste?
Is there a bridge or ford across this steam?	¿Hay un puente o vado a través de este arroyo?
How far is the nearest village?	¿A qué distancia está el próximo pueblo?
I am lost. Can you please direct me to . . . ?	Me he perdido. ¿Puede indicarme el camino a . . . ?
Will you please show me the route on this map?	¿Me puede enseñar el camino en este mapa, por favor?

VOCABULARY

barn	el granero
bird	el pájaro
brook	el arroyo
canal	el canal
cliff	el acantilado
cottage	el chalet
cow	la vaca
dog	el perro
farm	la granja
field	el prado
footpath	la senda
forest	el bosque
goat	la cabra
heath	el brezal

Motoring

hill	la colina
horse	el caballo
inn	el mesón
lake	el lago
marsh	el pantano
moorland	el páramo
mountain	la montaña
orchard	la huerta
peak	el pico
pond	el estanque
river	el río
sea	el mar
sheep	la oveja
spring	la fuente
stream	el arroyo
tree	el árbol
valley	el valle
village	el pueblo
vineyard	la viña
waterfall	la cascada
well	el pozo
wood	el bosque

Motoring

At the Frontier

Here is my log book.

   green card insurance.
   driving licence.

I have an international licence.

This is a translation of my British licence.

Aquí está mi certificado de matrícula.
   carta verde de seguro.
   carnet de conducir.

Tengo un carnet internacional.

Esta es una traducción de mi carnet británico.

This is a self-drive car. Here are the documents.	**Este es un coche alquilado. Aquí están los documentos.**
You want to open the boot?	**¿Quiere abrir el porta-equipajes?**
I arrived today.	**He llegado hoy.**
I am staying for two weeks.	**Me quedo dos semanas.**
We are passing through on the way to Portugal.	**Estamos de paso de camino a Portugal.**
Does this custom post close at night?	**¿Cierra por la noche este puesto de aduanas?**
At what time?	**¿A qué hora?**
Do you sell petrol coupons?	**¿Vende cupones de gasolina?**
Shall I leave my engine running?	**¿Dejo el motor en marcha?**
Do you want me to stop the engine?	**¿Quiere que pare el motor?**

On the Road

Spanish roads are classified as follows:

Autopista	A
National Route	N IV
Other Routes	N4
Country roads	C2

National roads are generally well surfaced but often narrow and it is difficult to overtake. Country roads are narrow and picturesque and if you are not in a hurry, and want to absorb the atmosphere of the region through which you are travelling, you may find them worthwhile.

Can you tell me how to get to Ronda?	**¿Puede decirme cómo se va a Ronda?**

How many kilometres is it?	¿Cuántos kilómetros hay?
Is it a good road?	¿Es una carretera buena?
Is it hilly/flat/straight/winding?	¿Es montañoso/llano/derecho/sinuoso?
What is the speed limit on this section?	¿Cuál es el límite de velocidad en este tramo?
Will you point out the route on this map please?	¿Me puede señalar la ruta en este mapa, por favor?
How much does this section of motorway cost?	¿Cuánto cuesta este tramo de la autopista?
Do I pay at the exit?	¿Pago a la salida?
I am sorry, I have no change.	Lo siento. No tengo cambio.
How far is it to the next petrol station?	¿A cuánto está la próxima gasolinera?
I want twenty-five litres, please.	Quiero veinticinco litros, por favor.
Give me 200 pesetas' worth.	Deme doscientas pesetas de valor.
Fill her up.	Llenela.
Please check the oil and water.	Por favor mire el aceite y el agua.
I need some air in the tyres.	Necesito aire en los neumáticos.
I think the windscreen fluid needs topping up.	Creo que el líquido del parabrisas necesita rellenar.
Have you any distilled water for the battery?	¿Tiene agua destilada para la batería?
Please clean the windscreen.	Por favor limpie el parabrisas.

Have you any paper towels?	**¿Tiene toallas de papel?**
Have you got a carwash?	**¿Tiene lavado de coches?**
Do you sell yellow filters for the headlights?	**¿Vende filtros amarillos para los faros?**
Can I park here?	**¿Puedo aparcar aquí?**
Where is the nearest car park?	**¿Dónde está el parque de automóviles más próximo?**

Trouble with the Police

Usually the police are polite and helpful to visitors, but they are more likely to be so if you appear friendly and cooperative. A few phrases in their language can sometimes work miracles.

I'm sorry. I did not see you signal.	**Lo siento. No le he visto indicar.**
I thought I had right of way.	**Creí que tenía el derecho de paso.**
I apologize. I won't do it again.	**Me disculpe. No lo volveré a hacer.**
Here is my name and address.	**Aquí está mi nombre y dirección.**
This is my passport.	**Este es mi pasaporte.**
Do I have to pay a fine?	**¿Tengo que pagar una multa?**
How much?	**¿Cuánto?**
I haven't got any cash on me. Can I settle up at a police station?	**No llevo dinero. ¿Puedo pagar en la comisaría?**
Thank you for your courtesy.	**Gracias por ser tan amable.**

Car Rental

I want to hire a small car.	**Quiero alquilar un coche pequeño.**
a family saloon.	**un turismo.**
a large car.	**un coche grande.**
a sports car.	**un deportivo.**
a van.	**una furgoneta.**
I shall need it for . . . days.	**Lo necesitaré por . . . días.**
How much is the daily charge?	**¿Cuánto cuesta por día?**
Is it cheaper by the week?	**¿Es más barato por semana?**
Does that include mileage and insurance?	**¿Incluye el kilometraje y el seguro?**
What is the mileage charge?	**¿Cuánto es por el kilometraje?**
Is the insurance for car and passengers?	**¿Es el seguro para el coche y los pasajeros?**
Where do I pick up the car?	**¿Dónde recojo el coche?**
Can you bring it to my hotel?	**¿Lo puede traer a mi hotel?**
Can I leave it at another town or at the airport?	**¿Puedo dejarlo en otra ciudad o en el aeropuerto?**
Is there a deposit to pay?	**¿Hay que pagar un depósito?**
May I pay with my credit card?	**¿Puedo pagar con mi tarjeta de crédito?**
Will you please check the documents with me?	**Por favor, ¿puede comprobar los documentos conmigo?**
Will you show me the gears and instrument panel?	**¿Me enseña la caja de guías y el cuadro de mandos?**
Is the tank full of petrol?	**¿Está el tanque lleno de gasolina?**

Road Signs

Aduana	Customs
Al paso	Slowly
Alto	Stop
Aparcamiento	Parking
Atención	Take care
Autopista	Motorway
Calzada deteriorada	Bad surface
Cañada	Road narrows
Carretera cortada	Road interrupted
Ceda el paso	Give way
Centro Urbano	City Centre
Cruce peligroso	Dangerous crossing
Cuidado	Take care
Curva peligrosa	Dangerous bend
Despacio	Slow
Desviación	Diversion
Dirección única	One way
Escuela	School
Estacionamiento prohibido reglamentado	Parking forbidden limited time
Obras	Road works
Paso a nivel	Level crossing
Peatones	Pedestrians
Prohibido adelantar	No overtaking
Zona azul	Parking zone (with limited time)

Trouble on the Road

OTHER PEOPLE'S

There has been an accident three miles back.	**Ha habido un accidente a cinco kilómetros de aquí.**

Will you phone the police please?	**¿Puede llamar a la policía, por favor?**
No, I did not see it happen.	**No, no he visto como ha sucedido.**
The car number was …	**El número del coche era …**
I do not think anyone is hurt.	**No creo que hay ningún herido.**
Someone is badly hurt.	**Alquien está malherido.**

Yours

Are you all right?	**¿Está usted bien?**
My passengers are not hurt.	**Mis pasajeros no están heridos.**
The car is damaged.	**Mi coche ha sufrido daños.**
May I have your insurance details?	**¿Me puede dar los detalles de su seguro?**
Your name and address please?	**¿Su nombre y dirección, por favor?**
Will you please fill out this form?	**¿Puede llenar esta hoja, por favor?**
I think we shall have to call the police.	**Creo que tendremos que llamar a la policía.**
Excuse me, would you mind being a witness?	**Perdone, ¿le importa ser testigo?**
It happened because he put his brakes on suddenly.	**Ha ocurrido porque aplicó el freno repentinamente.**
He came out of a side road without signalling.	**Salió de una calle secundaria sin hacer señal.**

He tried to overtake on a narrow stretch of road.	**Trató de adelantar en un trozo estrecho de la carretera.**
He turned off without signalling.	**Dió la vuelta sin hacer señal.**
May I explain to someone who understands English?	**¿Puedo explicarme a alguien que entienda el inglés?**

If you are unfortunate enough to have an accident, be sure to get all the details from the other driver involved. Your insurance company will have provided you with an accident report form. It is a wise precaution to take out a bail bond (**una fianza**) to avoid the possibility of imprisonment if you are involved in a road accident in Spain.

Breakdown

If you have a breakdown put the red triangle behind the car at once or you may be penalized.

Thank you for stopping. I am in trouble. Will you help me?	**Gracias por pararse. Estoy en un apuro. ¿Me puede ayudar?**
My car has broken down.	**Mi coche está averiado.**
Will you tell the next garage or breakdown service vehicle that you pass?	**¿Se lo puede decir al próximo garaje o taller de reparaciones que pase?**
Will you please telephone a garage for me?	**¿Puede telefonear a un garaje por mí, por favor?**
Can you give me a lift to the next telephone?	**¿Me puede llevar en su coche hasta el próximo teléfono?**
Can you send a breakdown truck?	**¿Puede enviar un camión de averías?**
I am five kilometres from the last entry.	**Estoy a cinco kilómetros de la última entrada.**

Motoring

I am three kilometres from Valencia on the N ...	**Estoy a tres kilómetros de Valencia en la N ...**
How long will you be?	**¿Cuánto tardará?**

Repairs

There's something wrong with the engine.	**Hay algo que no va bien en el motor.**
The clutch is slipping.	**El embrague está resbaladizo.**
There is a noise from the back.	**Hay un ruido en la parte de atrás.**
The brakes are not working.	**Los frenos no funcionan.**
The cooling system is leaking.	**El sistema de enfriamiento gotea.**
My fan belt is broken.	**La correa del ventilador está rota.**
I've got a flat tyre.	**Tengo un neumático pinchado.**
The electrical system has failed.	**El sistema eléctrico ha fallado.**
The engine is overheating.	**El motor calienta demasiado.**
The car won't start.	**El coche no arranca.**
What is the matter?	**¿Qué pasa?**

Is it broken?
  burnt out?
  disconnected?
  jammed?
  leaking?
  short circuiting?
	¿Está roto?
	  quemado?
	  desconectado?
	  atascado?
	  goteando?
	  fundido?

Do I need a new part?	**¿Necesito una pieza nueva?**
Is there a Ford agent in town?	**¿Hay un agente Ford en la ciudad?**
Can you send for the part?	**¿Puede pedir la pieza?**
Is it serious?	**¿Es grave?**
How long will it take to repair?	**¿Cuánto tiempo le llevará repararlo?**
Can I hire another car?	**¿Puedo alquilar otro coche?**
What will it cost?	**¿Cuánto costará?**
I will get the part flown from Britain.	**Haré que manden por avión la pieza desde Inglaterra.**
Your mechanic has been very kind; I would like to tip him.	**Su mecánico ha sido muy amable; me gustaría darle propina.**

VOCABULARY

battery	**la batería**
brakes	**los frenos**
brake lining	**la guarnición del freno**
bulbs	**las bombillas**
carburettor	**el carburador**
clutch	**el embrague**
cooling system	**el sistema de enfriamiento**
dip switch	**las luces bajas**
dynamo	**la dínamo**
distributor	**el distribuidor**
electrical system	**el sistema eléctrico**
engine	**el motor**
exhaust pipe	**el tubo de escape**
fan	**la ventilación**
filter	**el filtro**

fuel pump	**la bomba de gasolina**
fuel tank	**el depósito**
gears	**la caja de cambios**
generator	**el generador**
hand brake	**el freno de mano**
headlights	**las luces de cruce**
heating system	**la calefacción**
horn	**la bocina, el claxon**
ignition	**el encendido**
indicator	**el indicador**
lubrication system	**el sistema de lubrificación**
radiator	**el radiador**
reflectors	**los reflectores**
seat	**el asiento**
silencer	**el silenciador**
sparking plug	**la bujía**
speedometer	**el indicador de velocidad**
suspension	**la suspensión**
transmission	**la transmisión**
wheels	**las ruedas**
windscreen wipers	**el limpiaparabrisas**

A Place to Stay

There are places to stay to suit every budget level in Spain, from the first-class hotels of the beach resorts to simple pensions. If you have not booked a hotel in advance, ask at the tourist office of each town. They will help you find a place within your price range. If you don't want to stay at an hotel, there are apartments and camping sites and rooms in private houses. The standards of comfort vary considerably and cheap accommodation is often rather austere.

Hotels and Pensions

Finding a Room

I am travelling with the . . . Travel Agency.	Viajo con la Agencia . . .
Here is my hotel coupon.	Aquí está mi cupón para el hotel.
My room is already reserved.	Mi habitación está ya reservada.
I am travelling independently.	Viajo independientemente.
Will a porter bring my luggage in?	¿Me puede traer un mozo el equipaje?
Can I leave my car here?	¿Puedo dejar mi coche aquí?
Is there a car park?	¿Hay aparcamiento?
Are you the receptionist/ concierge/manager?	¿Es usted la recepcionista/el conserje/gerente?
Have you a single/double/three-bedded room?	¿Tiene una habitación sencilla/doble/de tres camas?

with a full-size bath and separate toilet?	con un baño grande y wáter separado?
with bath or shower?	con baño o ducha?
with a balcony?	con balcón?
looking over the front/the back?	con vistas adelante/atrás?

How much is it per day?

¿Cuánto es por día?

Is there a reduction for a longer stay/for children?

¿Hay reducción por una estancia más larga/por niños?

Are there special mealtimes for children?

¿Hay horas de comer especiales para niños?

I don't want to pay more than ... pesetas per day.

No quiero pagar mas de ... pesetas por día.

Have you anything cheaper?

¿Tiene algo más barato?

Do I have to fill in a visitor's card?

¿Debo de rellenar una tarjeta de visitas?

Here is my passport.

Aquí está mi pasaporte.

How long will you keep it?

¿Cuánto tiempo lo tendrá?

I'd like to go up to my room right away.

Me gustaría ir a mi habitación inmediatamente.

Will you send up the luggage?

¿Me subirá el equipaje?

This case is for Room 3 and that one for Number 12.

Esta maleta es para la habitación tres y la otra para el número doce.

May I have the room key?

¿Me da la llave de la habitación?

Is the key in the door?

¿Está la llave en la puerta?

Where is the lift?

¿Dónde está el ascensor?

Do I work it myself?	¿Lo hago funcionar yo mismo/misma?
Do you do bed and breakfast/demi pension?	¿Dan cama y desayuno/media pensión?
Can I put all extras on my bill?	¿Puedo poner todos los extras en mi cuenta?
Is there a post box in the hotel?	¿Hay un buzón en el hotel?
Can you get the daily papers for me?	¿Puede obtener los diarios para mí?

Moving In

This room is too small/large/noisy/dark/high up.	Esta habitación es demasiado pequeña/grande/ruidosa/obscura/alta.
You haven't got a double bed?	¿No tiene una cama doble?
Please make the twin beds into one double.	Por favor, convierta las dos camas en una doble.
I need a child's cot.	Necesito una cuna de niño.
I shall need another pillow/blanket/clothes hanger some writing paper.	Necesitaré otra almohada/manta/percha. papel de escribir.
The bedside light is not working.	La luz del lado de la cama no funciona.
The bulb is broken.	La bombilla está fundida.
Which is the hot tap/the cold?	¿Cual es el grifo del agua caliente/de la fría?
Is this the electric razor socket?	¿Es este el enchufe de la máquina de afeitar?
What is the voltage?	¿Cuál es el voltaje?

Accommodation

My plug won't fit.	Mi clavija no sirve.
Have you got an adaptor?	¿Tiene un adaptador?
Is there an electrician in the village?	¿Hay un electricista en el pueblo?
Is there a hotel laundry/facilities for washing and ironing clothes?	¿Hay lavandería en el hotel/facilidades para lavar y planchar la ropa?
The blind is stuck.	La persiana está trabada.
Will you bring a bottle of drinking water?	¿Puede traer una botella de agua potable?
Can I leave valuables in the hotel safe?	¿Puedo dejar mis valores en la caja fuerte del hotel
What time is breakfast/lunch/dinner?	¿A qué hora es el desayuno/la comida/cena?
Do you serve breakfast in bed?	¿Sirven desayuno en la habitación?
Does the hotel do packed lunches?	¿Hace el hotel comidas empaquetadas?

Small Hotels and Pensions

Do you have set times for meals?	¿Tiene horas especiales para las comidas?
May I have a towel and soap?	¿Me puede dar una toalla y jabón?
At what time do you lock the front door at night?	¿A qué hora cierra la puerta por la noche?
May I have a key?	¿Me da la llave?
Is it all right to leave the car in the street?	¿Está bien si dejo el coche en la calle?

Will our things be safe?	¿Estarán nuestras cosas a salvo?
Where is the nearest garage?	¿Cuál es el garaje más cercano?

Rooms in Private Houses

Do you have a room free?	¿Tiene una habitación libre?
Do you do breakfast?	¿Dan desayuno?
Is there a café nearby?	¿Hay un café cerca?
Would you like me to pay now?	¿Quiere que pague ahora?
At what time will it be convenient to use the bathroom?	¿A qué hora le viene bien que use el baño?
Do I need to tell you if I have a bath?	¿Se lo tengo que decir si me doy un baño?
Could you wake us in the morning?	¿Nos puede despertar a la mañana?
Is there a lounge?	¿Hay un salón?
Shall I lock my room?	¿Cierro mi puerta con llave?

Paying the Bill

May I have my bill, please?	¿Me da la cuenta, por favor?
Will you prepare my bill for first thing tomorrow?	¿Me preparará la cuenta para mañana a primera hora?
I think there is a mistake.	Creo que hay un error.
I don't understand this item.	No entiendo este detalle.
May I pay by cheque?	¿Puedo pagar con cheque?

Accommodation

Yes, I have a Eurocheque card.	**Si, tengo una tarjeta Eurocheque.**
Do you accept credit cards?	**¿Aceptan tarjetas de crédito?**
Is service included?	**¿Está incluido el servicio?**
Is tax included?	**¿Están incluidas las tasas?**
May I have a receipt, please?	**¿Me da un recibo, por favor?**
Please forward my mail to ...	**Por favor, remita mi correspondencia a ...**
We have enjoyed ourselves very much.	**Lo hemos disfrutado mucho.**
May I have one of your leaflets?	**¿Me da uno de sus folletos?**

VOCABULARY

bar	**el bar**
barman	**el barman**
bed	**la cama**
chair	**la silla**
chambermaid	**la sirvienta**
children's playground	**el patio de recreo de niños**
discotheque	**la discoteca**
door	**la puerta**
hall	**el vestíbulo**
lift	**el ascensor**
lounge	**el salón**
light switch	**el interruptor de la luz**
luggage porter	**el mozo de equipaje**
manager	**el gerente**
mirror	**el espejo**
night club	**el club de noche**

playground	el patio
playroom	el cuarto de los niños
radio	la radio
restaurant	el restaurante
stairs	las escaleras
swimming pool	la piscina
telephone operator	la telefonista
waiter	el camarero
waitress	la camarera
wardrobe	el armario
window	la ventana

Catering for Yourself

Villas and Apartments

I have booked a villa/apartment.	He reservado una villa/un piso.
Here is my voucher.	Aquí está mi vale.
Will you please show me around?	Por favor ¿me lo enseña?
Where is the light switch/power point/fuse box?	¿Dónde está el interruptor/el enchufe/la caja del plomo?
Do all the outside doors lock?	¿Cierran con llave todas las puertas exteriores?
How do the shutters work?	¿Cómo funcionan las contraventanas?
Will you show me the hot water system?	¿Me puede enseñar el sistema del agua caliente?
Where is the mains valve?	¿Dónde está la válvula de la cañería?

Catering for Yourself

Is there mains gas?	¿Hay cañería del gas?
Are gas cylinders delivered?	¿Reparten los cilindros de gas?
At what time does the house help come?	¿A qué hora viene la muchacha?
Can we have three sets of house keys?	¿Nos puede dar tres conjuntos de llaves de la casa?
When is the rubbish collected?	¿Cuándo recogen la basura?
Are the shops nearby?	¿Hay tiendas cerca?
Where is the bus stop/station?	¿Dónde está la parada de autobús/estación?
Have you a map of the resort?	¿Tiene un mapa del lugar?

Camping

Have you a site free?	¿Tiene un sitio libre?
Do you rent bungalows?	¿Alquila chalets?
tents?	tiendas de campaña?
cooking equipment?	equipo de cocina?
Are there toilets?	¿Hay wáter?
washing facilities?	facilidades para lavarse?
cooking facilities?	facilidades para cocinar?
How much does it cost per night?	¿Cuánto cuesta por noche?
Can I put my tent here?	¿Puedo poner mi tienda aquí?
Is there room for a trailer?	¿Hay espacio para un remolque?
Is there a night guard?	¿Hay un guarda de noche?

Where is the camp shop?	¿Dónde está la tienda del 'camping'?
restaurant?	el restaurante?
the nearest shopping centre?	el centro comercial más cercano?
At what time do we have to vacate the site?	¿A qué hora tenemos que dejar vacante el sitio?
Where is the drinking tap?	¿Dónde está el grifo del agua potable?

VOCABULARY

barbecue	la barbacoa
basin	la jofaina
bucket	el cubo
camping gas	el gas butano
frame tent	la armazón de la tienda
grill	la parrilla
guyropes	las cuerdas
ice-bucket	el cubo de hielo
insecticide	el insecticida
knife	el cuchillo
mosquito repellant	el repelente de mosquitos
penknife	la navaja
sleeping bag	el saco de dormir
spade	la pala
stove	el hornillo
tent	la tienda de campaña
tent peg	la estaquilla
waterproof sheet	la sábana impermeable

Catering for Yourself

Youth Hostelling

Is there a youth hostel in this town?	**¿Hay un albergue de la juventud en esta ciudad?**
Have you room for tonight?	**¿Tiene cama para esta noche?**
We are members of the Youth Hostel Association.	**Somos miembros de la Sociedad de Albergues Juveniles.**
What are the house rules?	**¿Cuales son las reglas del albergue?**
How long can we stay?	**¿Cuánto nos podemos quedar?**
Is there a youth hostel at . . .?	**¿Hay un albergue en . . .?**

Eating and Drinking

Meal times not only offer a chance to satisfy the appetite, but provide an intimate glimpse of the life of the places you are visiting. There are the regional specialities to savour, which reveal something of the character of the local environment. The dishes of the Basque country, for example, differ considerably from those of Andalusia. In the former there is young lamb and kid, while in the south, along the coast, there are fish and citrus fruits.

Above all, meal times provide an opportunity to watch the fascinating drama of people: the farmers at the village **fonda**, the families at Sunday lunch, the fishermen at the quayside café. Different types of restaurant satisfy different tastes and there is a wide variety.

At bars you can buy drinks and **tapas** (a variety of appetizer). **Cafeterías** serve drinks and there is a self-service counter. **Hosterías** are restaurants with regional cooking and a **fonda** is an inn. **Paradors** are state-run hotels with restaurants and are often situated in historic buildings.

Spain is not a rich agricultural country and rich dishes are not abundant. Nevertheless there is much to enjoy, especially the fresh fish which can be obtained along the coast. Meal times in Spain are late; lunch is served from 13.00 to 15.00 and dinner from 20.30 to midnight.

Can you recommend a good restaurant?	**¿Puede recomendar un buen restaurante?**
one that is not too expensive?	**uno que no sea demasiado caro?**
a typical restaurant of the region?	**un restaurante típico de la región?**
one with music?	**uno con música?**
a four star establishment?	**un establecimiento con cuatro estrellas?**

Eating and Drinking

a Chinese/Italian/French/Basque/Galician/Andalusian restaurant.	un restaurante chino/italiano/francés/vasco/gallego/andaluz?
Is there a good snack bar nearby?	¿Hay cerca un buen bar?
Where can I find a self-service restaurant?	¿Dónde puedo encontrar un autoservicio?
Do I need to reserve a table?	¿Necesito reservar una mesa?
I'd like a table for two at nine o'clock.	Me gustaría una mesa para dos a las nueve.
not too near the door/the orchestra.	no demasiado cerca de la puerta/la orquesta.
in the corner.	en la esquina.
away from the kitchen.	a distancia de la cocina.

At the Restaurant

A table for four, please.	Una mesa para cuatro, por favor.
Is this our table?	¿Es esta nuestra mesa?
This table will do fine.	Esta mesa está bien.
The tablecloth is dirty.	El mantel está sucio.
The table is unsteady.	La mesa se menea.
The ashtray is missing.	Falta el cenicero.
May I see the menu?	¿Puedo ver el menú?
We will have an aperitif while we look at it.	Tomaremos un aperitivo mientras lo miramos.
Please bring the wine list.	Por favor, traiga la lista de vinos.

Have you got a set menu?	**¿Tiene un menú fijo?**
What do you recommend today?	**¿Qué recomienda hoy?**
What does it consist of?	**¿De qué consiste?**
It sounds good. I'll try it.	**Parece bueno. Lo probaré.**
The soup is cold. Please warm it up.	**La sopa está fría. Por favor, caliéntela.**
This fork is dirty. May I have a clean one?	**Este tenedor está sucio. ¿Me puede dar uno limpio?**
Will you call our waiter?	**¿Puede llamar a nuestro camarero?**
We did not order this.	**No pedimos esto.**
I'd like to speak to the head waiter.	**Quisiera hablar con el jefe.**
My compliments to the chef.	**Saludos al cocinero.**
It's very good.	**Es muy bueno.**
Have you any house wine?	**¿Tiene vino de la casa?**
I'd like a half bottle/a carafe.	**Me gustaría media botella/una garrafa.**
Which is the local wine?	**¿Cuál es el vino local?**
This wine is corked.	**Este vino sabe a corcho.**
The children will share a portion.	**Los niños compartirán una porción.**
May we have some water?	**¿Me puede traer agua?**
Have you any mineral water?	**¿Tiene agua mineral?**
Have you a high chair for the child?	**¿Tiene una silla alta para el niño?**
Where are the toilets?	**¿Dónde están los lavabos?**

The Menu

Menus will vary from place to place. Most restaurants display
them outside and offer set meals from a simple menu for
tourists to the **menú gastronómico** for the gourmet. There
is usually a service charge added to the bill, but you are
expected to leave a little extra.

Tapas

This is the name given to a variety of small dishes offered by
bars where Spaniards congregate before meals, especially in
the evening. The aperitif hour is a social occasion and
everyone has their favourite bar where they meet their
friends. **Tapas** range from little plates of olives to shellfish
and cold meats and are almost a meal in themselves for people
with small appetites.

aceitunas	olives
aguacate	avocado
albóndigas	meat balls
alcachofa	artichoke
almejas	clams
anchoas	anchovies
anguila ahumada	smoked eels
banderillas	savouries on sticks
buñuelitos	fritters, usually of ham or fish
calamares a la Romana	deep fried squid
calamares en su tinta	squid in their ink
callos	tripe
caracoles	snails

champiñones	mushrooms
chorizo	cured sausage with garlic
cigalas	crayfish
gambas a la plancha	prawns grilled with garlic
langostinos	large prawns
mejillones	mussels
ostras	oysters
percebes	goose barnacles
pepinillos	gherkins
sardinas	sardines

Starters

Some of the **tapas** will also appear as starters on restaurant menus but here are some more dishes that you will come across

cabeza de ternera	jellied calf's head
cangrejo	crab
espárragos	asparagus
fiambres	cold meats
huevos a la Flamenca	eggs with tomatoes, ham and onions
jamon Serrano	cured ham
mayonesa de huevos	egg mayonnaise, supposed to be named after Mahon on the island of Minorca
tortilla	omelette – there is a wide variety of fillings for these: cheese, shellfish, sausage, etc.

Eating and Drinking

Soups

calderada	a Galician fish soup
cocido madrileño	rich meat and vegetable soup or stew
consomé al Jerez	consommé with sherry
gazpacho Andaluz	ice-cold soup of garlic, onions, tomatoes and peppers
sopa de ajo	garlic soup
sopa de albóndigas Catalana	meat ball soup from Catalonia
sopa de almendras	almond soup
sopa de cuarto de hora	quarter-hour soup made of shellfish, onions and tomatoes
sopa de fideos	noodle soup
sopa de tomates	tomato soup

Fish

arroz a la Valenciana	Spanish rice with shellfish
anchoas en cazuela	fresh anchovy stew
bacalao a la Vizcaina	cod in Basque style
besugo a la Donostiarra	bream with garlic and lemon
buñuelo de Bacalao	cod fritters
calamares rellenos	stuffed squid
calderete Asturiano	Asturian fish stew
chanquetes	whitebait
filete de lenguado	sole fillet
langostinos a la Catalana	crayfish Catalan style

68

lenguado a la Andaluza	sole with aubergine, tomatoes and peppers
lubina al horno	baked bass
merluza	hake
pez espada en amarillo	swordfish with saffron
raya en pimentón	skate with peppers
truchas Felipe	trout fried with ham and bacon
zarzuela de mariscos	seafood stew

Meat

Beef is generally speaking rather tough in Spain and in most other mountainous countries of the Spanish-speaking world, but veal is good and in the northern provinces of Spain young lamb is excellent. Kid is also eaten and is something of a delicacy; so, too, is sucking pig.

biftec	steak
calderete Extremadura de cabrito	kid stew Extremadura style
carne picada	minced meat
cazuela a la Catalana	minced beef with sausage
chuletas a la parrilla	grilled chops
cochifrito	fricassée of lamb
cochinillo asado	roast sucking pig
cocido Andaluz	meat stew with chick peas and sausage Andalusian style
cordero en ajillo pastor	lamb in casserole with paprika
escalopes de ternera labrador	veal sandwiched between ham and fried in butter

estofado de vaca	beef stew
filete	fillet
hígado a la Asturiana	liver with almonds
lengua Aragonesa	tongue with vegetables
pimientos a la Riojana	peppers stuffed with minced meat
pote Gallego	Galician stew with steak, ham and sausages
riñones de Cordero a la señorita	kidneys with ham, onions and sauce espagnole
salchichas	sausages: there is a wide variety both fresh and cured. Among these are Butifarra, made from fat pork and spices; Longaniza, made with lean pork and herbs; Mortadela, made with lean pork with cubes of fat and spices; Morcilla, a black sausage, and Salchichón, a pork sausage with bacon.
sesos fritos	brains (fried)

Cooking Methods and Sauces

ahumado	smoked
a la Catalana	with tomatoes and green peppers
a la parrilla	grilled
a la Romana	deep fried
a la Vasca	with parsley, peas and garlic
al horno	baked

al vapor	steamed
en escabeche	marinated
estofado	braised
frito	fried
hervido	boiled
muy hecho	well done
poco hecho	rare (steak)
regular	medium
salteado	saute

Game and Fowl

Chicken is used extensively in Spain and forms the basis of a wide variety of dishes.

codorniz en tomate	quails in tomato sauce
gallina en pepitoria	hen in casserole with almonds and saffron
liebre en estofado	stewed hare
pastel de conejo	rabbit pie
pavo adobado	marinated turkey in casserole
perdíz en estofado	partridge stew
pollo a la cacerola	casseroled chicken
puchero de gallina	stewed chicken

Vegetables

Spaniards do not eat many specially prepared vegetable dishes and most vegetables are eaten as an accompaniment to the main dish. Here are a few special preparations you may find on a menu, as well as ordinary vegetables.

alcachofas	artichokes
berenjenas rellenas	stuffed aubergines
cacheles	potatoes with green cabbage and chorizo sausage
calabacines rellenos	stuffed courgettes
cebolla	onion
champiñones	mushrooms
col	cabbage
guisantes	peas
habas a la Rondeña	broad beans Ronda style (with ham and boiled eggs)
judías verdes	green beans
lechuga	lettuce
menestra de espinaca	spinach and eggs
pepino	cucumber
pimientos	peppers
pisto	a Spanish ratatouille
puerros	leeks
tomates	tomatoes
torta de acelgas	beet spinach tart
zanahorias	carrots

Desserts

Generally speaking, meals in Spain finish with fruit, though tourist hotels will include some of the usual desserts which are internationally recognized. Here are some ordinary as well as some essentially Spanish desserts that you may come across.

arroz con leche	rice pudding
bizcochos de avellana	hazelnut biscuits
borrachitos	tipsy cake
buñuelitos de San José	rice fritters
crema de Málaga	Malaga cream
crema Catalana	caramel pudding
dulce de membrillo	quince jelly
flan	caramel pudding
helado	ice cream
melocotón en almíbar	peaches in syrup
pastel	cake
pastel de queso	cheesecake
pastelitos de miel	honey fritters
piña	pineapple (tinned)
tarta de almendras	almond tart
tarta de manzana	apple tart
torta de miel y nueces	honey and nut cake
turrón	nougat

Cheeses

Burgos	This is a soft, mild cheese from the north of Spain.
Bola	A round-shaped, mild cheese not unlike Dutch Edam.
Cabra	A goat cheese; there are various types, some stronger than others.
Mahón	A cheese from the Balearic Islands.
Manchego	A hard rich cheese from La Mancha, Don Quixote's home.
Perilla	A bland white cheese.
Roncal	This cheese comes from northern Spain. It is made from ewe's milk and is salted and cured.
Villalón	Made from curdled ewe's milk.

Fruit

albaricoques	apricots
cerezas	cherries
ciruelas	plums
ensalada de fruta	fruit salad
frambuesas	raspberries
fresas	strawberries
granadas	pomegranites
grosellas	redcurrants

higos	figs
mandarinas	tangerines
manzanas	apples
melocotones	peaches
melón	melon
naranjas	oranges
peras	pears
piña	pineapple
plátano	banana
uvas	grapes

Drinks

Aperitifs and wine are part of the way of life of Spanish-speaking countries, and as a rule vermouth is the most popular aperitif. Naturally, there are many brands of sherry available, and the ones well known abroad such as Tio Pepe, Dry Sack and La Ina can be found everywhere. Spaniards also drink sherry-type wines.

Spain produces a number of good versions of French liqueurs under special licence and there are also liqueurs of Spanish origin such as Calisay, Triple Seco, Crema de Cacao and Anis.

Will you bring me a sherry, please?	**¿Me trae un jerez, por favor?**
A vermouth with ice and lemon, please.	**Un vermut con hielo y limón, por favor.**

I'll have my scotch on the rocks.
    with soda water.
    with plain water.
	Tomaré mi whisky con hielo.
	    con sifón.
	    con agua natural.

75

Eating and Drinking

| Have you any non-alcoholic drinks? | ¿Tiene bebidas no alcohólicas? |

dry	seco
medium	mediano
sherry	jerez
sweet	dulce
vermouth	vermut

Wine

As in most Latin countries, wine is drunk by almost everybody at meals and as an aperitif. Sometimes it is mixed with soda water or made into a **sangría**, a chilled punch with citrus fruits, wine and lemonade. Spanish wine is mostly table wine and does not aspire to the vintage classifications which are a guide to a good wine in France. Nevertheless there are some excellent Spanish wines, chief among which are the Marques de Riscal and Marques de Murrieta, both from the famous Rioja vineyards in the valley of the Ebro in Northern Spain. Other wine names to look out for are Bodegas Bilbainas, Federico Paternina and Bodegas Franco-Españolas. Valdepeñas is another good wine-producing area south of Madrid. Here the wine produced is lighter and much drunk as a table wine in Madrid.

Spanish white wines from these regions are very pleasant to drink. They range from a Rhine type (Cepa Rhin) to a dry Chablis, and Spanish champagne is also produced in large quantities.

Sweet wines are produced south of Barcelona at Tarragona and further south in Málaga.

Soft drinks

May we have some tea, please?	¿Nos puede servir té, por favor?
a pot of tea?	una tetera llena?
lemon/China/Indian tea?	un té con limón/té chino/té indio?
a coffee with milk/cream?	un café con leche/crema?
a black/iced coffee?	un café negro/helado?
Have you any lemonade?	¿Tiene limonada?
I'd like a long, cool drink with plenty of ice.	Quisiera una bebida larga refrescante con bien de hielo.
an orange juice with soda water.	un zumo de naranja con sifón.
a glass of cold milk.	un vaso de leche fría.
Have you a straw?	¿Tiene una pajita?
Do you make milk shakes?	¿Hace batidos de leche?
Have you a bottle with a screw top?	¿Tiene una botella con rosca?

VOCABULARY

beef tea	el jugo de carne
canned beer	la cerveza en lata
chocolate	el chocolate
cordial	el cordial
cup	la taza
ginger ale	la cerveza de jengibre
lager	la cerveza
syphon	el sifón
tonic	la tónica
tumbler	el vaso

Shopping

Buying Food

Eating out is fun but so is buying food in the various food shops and markets. The Spaniards set great store by freshness and quality and buying food is an important operation involving much discussion about the product.

At the Butcher's

What kind of meat is that?	¿Qué clase de carne es esa?
What do you call that cut?	¿Cómo llama esa parte?
I'd like some steaks, please.	Quisiera bistecs, por favor.
How much does that weigh?	¿Cuánto pesa eso?
Will you please trim off the fat?	¿Puede recortar el gordo, por favor?
Will you take the meat off the bone?	¿Puede remover la carne del hueso?
Will you mince it?	¿Puede picarla?
Please slice it very fine/thick.	Por favor, cortela en rodajas finas/gruesas.
Will you chine the cutlets?	¿Puede cortar las chuletas?
I'll have a little more.	Ponga un poco más.
That's too much.	Eso es demasiado.
Put it in a plastic bag.	Pongala en una bolsa de plástico.
Cut it in cubes.	Cortela en tajadas.

VOCABULARY

bacon	**tocino**
beef, pot roast	**carne de vaca para asar en tartera**
rib	**costilla**
rumpsteak	**filete de lomo**
filet	**filete**
roast beef	**para asar al horno**
sirloin	**solomillo**
brains	**los sesos**
cooking fat	**la manteca**
cutlets	**las chuletas**
escalope	**el escalope**
kidneys	**los riñones**
lamb, shoulder	**el cordero, la espalda**
leg	**la pierna**
liver	**el hígado**
pig's trotters	**la pata de cerdo**
pork, hand of	**cerdo, mano de**
leg	**la pierna**
chop	**la chuleta**
sausages	**las salchichas**
sweetbreads	**las lechecillas**

At the Fishmonger's

Will you clean the fish?	**¿Puede limpiar el pescado?**
Leave/take off the head/tail/fins.	**Deje/quite la cabeza/la cola/ las aletas.**
Have you any shellfish?	**¿Tiene mariscos?**
What is the name of that fish?	**¿Cómo se llama ese pescado?**

Buying Food

anchovies	**las anchoas**
bass	**la lubina**
bream	**el besugo**
carp	**la carpa**
clams	**las almejas**
cod	**el bacalao**
crab	**el cangrejo**
crayfish	**los langostinos**
eel	**la anguila**
herring	**el arenque**
lobster	**la langosta**
mullet	**el mújol**
mussels	**los mejillones**
octopus	**el pulpo**
oysters	**las ostras**
perch	**la perca**
pike	**el lucio**
plaice	**la platija**
prawns	**las gambas**
salmon	**el salmón**
sardines	**las sardinas**
sole	**el lenguado**
squid	**los calamares**
trout	**la trucha**
tunny	**el atún**
turbot	**el rodaballo**
whitebait	**el boquerón**

At the Delicatessen/Dairy

What kinds of sausage have you got?

¿Qué clases de salchicha tiene?

I'd like one which is mild/peppery/without garlic.	Me gustaría una dulce/una picante/sin ajo.
May I see your selection of pâtés?	¿Puedo ver su selección de pastelillos?
I prefer a coarse pâté/smooth pâté/game pâté.	Prefiero uno basto/uno fino/uno de caza.
What is the name of that cheese?	¿Cuál es el nombre de ese queso?
Have you any goat's cheese?	¿Tiene queso de cabra?
Do I have to take the whole cheese or will you cut it?	¿Me tengo que llevar el queso entero o lo corta en trozos?
May I test it for ripeness?	¿Puedo mirar si está maduro?
Have you any biscuits/tea biscuits?	¿Tiene bizcochos/galletas María?
Do you sell breakfast cereals?	¿Vende cereales para el desayuno?
I'll take a little of each salad.	Me ponga un poco de cada ensalada.
Have you a tube of tomato puree?	¿Tiene un tubo de puré de tomate?
Have you a jar of olives?	¿Tiene un tarro de aceitunas?

VOCABULARY

anchovies	las anchoas
garlic sausage	el chorizo
gherkins	los pepinillos

Buying Food

ham	el jamón
macaroni	los macarrones
olives	las aceitunas
pâté de foie	el foiegras
pickles	el escabeche
salami	el salchichón
salt beef	la carne de vaca salada
smoked fish	el pescado ahumado
spaghetti	los fideos
stuffed olives	las aceitunas rellenas
tinned food	la comida en lata

AT THE GROCER'S/SUPERMARKET

bacon	el tocino
biscuits	los bizcochos
bottle (of)	la botella (de)
bread	el pan
butter	la mantequilla
cereals	los cereales
crisps	las patatas fritas
dried fruit	la fruta seca
eggs	los huevos
flour	la harina
garlic	el ajo
jam	la mermelada
jar (of)	el tarro (de)
margarine	la margarina
oil	el aceite
pepper	el pimiento
rice	el arroz
salt	la sal
tin (of)	la lata (de)
vinegar	el vinagre

At the Greengrocer's and Fruiterer's

Is the melon ripe?	¿Está maduro el melón?
How many/much will make a kilo?	¿Cuántos(as)/cuánto harán un kilo?
It's for eating today/tomorrow.	Es para comer hoy/mañana.
Will you please weigh this bunch?	¿Puede pesar este manojo, por favor?
This lettuce is rather limp.	Esta lechuga está bastante lacia.
Are these apples crisp?	¿Son crujientes estas manzanas?
Have you got a stronger bag?	¿Tiene una bolsa más fuerte?
I will put it in my carrier.	Lo pondré en mi bolsa de papel.
Have you got a box?	¿Tiene una caja?

VOCABULARY

apples	las manzanas
apricots	los albaricoques
artichoke	la alcachofa
asparagus	los espárragos
banana	el plátano
beans,	las alubias,
broad	las habas
French	los fríjoles
runner	las judías
beetroot	la remolacha
blackberry	la zarzamora
broccoli	el brécol
cabbage	la berza

carrots	**las zanahorias**
cauliflower	**la coliflor**
cherries	**las cerezas**
chestnut	**la castaña**
cress	**el berro**
cucumber	**el pepino**
date	**el dátil**
fig	**el higo**
grapefruit	**el pomelo**
grapes	**las uvas**
greengages	**las ciruelas claudias**
hazelnuts	**las avellanas**
leeks	**los puerros**
lemons	**los limones**
lettuce	**la lechuga**
melon	**el melón**
onions	**las cebollas**
oranges	**las naranjas**
peaches	**los melocotones**
pears	**las peras**
peas	**los guisantes**
pineapple	**la piña**
plums	**las ciruelas**
potatoes	**las patatas**
radishes	**los rábanos**
raspberries	**las frambuesas**
rhubarb	**el ruibarbo**
spinach	**la espinaca**
strawberries	**las fresas**
sweet corn	**el maiz tierno**
sweet pepper	**el pimiento**
tangerines	**las mandarinas**
tomatoes	**los tomates**
turnips	**los nabos**

Other Shops

Shopping is a pleasure anywhere, and in Spain there are many well-produced local goods. Leather, ceramics and lace are all worth buying. Most shops are open from 09.00 to 13.00 and 16.00 to 20.00, and even later in summer.

I want to go shopping. Where are the best shops?	**Quiero ir de compras. ¿Dónde están las mejores tiendas?**
the shops where everyone goes?	**las tiendas donde van todos?**
the cheaper shops?	**las tiendas más baratas?**
Where is the market?	**¿Dónde está el mercado?**
Till what time are you open?	**¿Hasta que hora está abierto?**
Is there a grocer near here?	**¿Hay una tienda de comestibles cerca de aquí?**

---

antique shop	**la tienda de antigüedades**
art gallery	**el museo**
baker	**la panadería**
bank	**el banco**
beauty salon	**el salón de belleza**
bookshop	**la librería**
butcher	**la carnicería**
chemist	**la farmacia**
confectioner	**la confitería**
dairy	**la lechería**
delicatessen	**la charcutería**
department store	**el almacén**

Shopping

dry cleaner	**la tintorería**
fishmonger	**la pescadería**
greengrocer	**la verdulería**
grocer	**los comestibles**
hairdresser	**la peluquería**
hardware store	**la ferretería**
jeweller	**la joyería**
newsagent	**el vendedor de periódicos**
off licence	**la tienda de licores**
optician	**el óptico**
photographer	**el fotógrafo**
shoemaker	**el zapatero**
shoe shop	**la zapatería**
stationer	**la papelería**
tailor	**el sastre**
tobacconist	**el estanco**
toy shop	**la tienda de juguetes**
travel agent	**la agencia de viajes**
watchmaker	**la relojería**
wine merchant	**el vinatero**

Buying Clothes

I'm just looking, thank you.	**Estoy mirando, gracias.**
I would like to look at some shirts.	**Me gustaría ver camisas.**
plain/coloured/striped.	**sencillas/de color/rayadas.**
with long/short sleeves.	**de manga larga/corta.**
in cotton.	**de algodón.**
My size is ...	**Mi talla es ...**
My collar size is ...	**El número de mi cuello es ...**
My waist/bust/hip size is ...	**Mido ... de cintura/pecho/ cadera.**

This colour does not suit me.	**Este color no me va bien.**
Have you something in wool/in red?	**¿Tiene algo en lana/en rojo?**
It is not my style.	**No es de mi estilo.**
I want something more casual.	**Quiero algo más de sport.**
Is there a fitting room where I can try it on?	**¿Hay una sala de pruebas donde me lo pueda poner?**
Can I return it if it is unsuitable?	**¿Lo puedo devolver si no me va bien?**
May I have a receipt?	**¿Me puede dar un recibo?**
It does not fit.	**No me sienta bien.**
It is too large/small/narrow/wide.	**Es demasiado grande/pequeño/estrecho/ancho.**
Can you show me something else?	**¿Me puede enseñar otra cosa?**
The zip is stuck/broken.	**La cremallera se ha trabado/roto.**

VOCABULARY

MATERIALS

camel hair	**el pelo de camello**
chiffon	**la gasa**
cotton	**el algodón**
crepe	**el crepé**
denim	**el dril**
felt	**el fieltro**
flannel	**la franela**
gabardine	**la gabardina**
lace	**el encaje**

leather	**el cuero**
linen	**el lino**
nylon	**el nilón**
pique	**el piqué**
poplin	**el popelín**
rayon	**el rayón**
satin	**el raso**
silk	**la seda**
suede	**el ante**
taffeta	**el tafetán**
tweed	**el tweed**
velour	**el aterciopelado**
velvet	**el terciopelo**
wool	**la lana**
worsted	**el estambre**

MEASUREMENTS

arm	**el brazo**
chest	**el pecho**
hip	**la cadera**
leg	**la pierna**
neck	**el cuello**
waist	**la cintura**

COLOURS

black	**negro**
blue	**azul**
green	**verde**
mauve	**malva**
pastel colours	**los colores pastel**
orange	**naranja**
red	**rojo**
rose	**rosa**
strong colours	**los colores fuertes**
violet	**violeta**
white	**blanco**
yellow	**amarillo**

ITEMS OF CLOTHING

anorak	el anorak
bathing hat	el gorro de baño
bathing suit	el traje de baño
bathrobe	el albornoz
belt	el cinturón
blazer	la chaqueta sport
blouse	la blusa
boots	las botas
bra	el sostén
briefs	los calzoncillos
buckle	la hebilla
button	el botón
cap	la gorra
cardigan	la chaqueta de punto
coat	el abrigo
cufflinks	los gemelos
dinner jacket	el smoking
dress	el vestido
dressing gown	la bata
elastic	la goma
evening dress	el traje de noche
girdle	la faja
gloves	los guantes
gym shoes	los zapatos de gimnasia
handkerchief	el pañuelo
hat	el sombrero
jacket	la chaqueta
jeans	los pantalones vaqueros
jumper	el jersey
machintosh	el impermeable
negligé	el salto de cama
nightdress	el camisón
overcoat	el abrigo
panties	las bragas
pants suit	el traje pantalón
pocket	el bolsillo

Shopping

press stud	el cierre
pullover	el jersey
pyjamas	los pijamas
raincoat	la gabardina
sandals	las sandalias
scarf	la bufanda, el pañuelo de cabeza
shirt	la camisa
shoelaces	los cordones de zapatos
shoes	los zapatos
shorts	los pantalones cortos
skirt	la falda
slip	la combinación
slippers	las zapatillas
socks	los calcetines
stockings	las medias
suit	el traje
suspenders	el liguero
swimsuit	el traje de baño
t-shirt	la camiseta
thread	el hilo
tie	la corbata
tights	los leotardos
trousers	los pantalones
twinset	el conjunto
underpants	los calzoncillos
vest	la camiseta
waistcoat	el chaleco
zip	la cremallera

At the Shoe Shop

I want a pair of walking shoes.	**Quiero un par de zapatos.**
evening shoes.	**zapatos de noche.**
moccasins.	**mocasines.**
boots.	**botas.**

suede shoes.	zapatos de ante.
slippers.	zapatillas.
sandals.	sandalias.
canvas shoes.	zapatos de lona.

My size is . . .

Mi número es . . .

I like a broad/narrow fitting.

Quisiera de horma ancha/estrecha.

I want high/low heels.

Quiero tacón alto/bajo.

I want flat-heeled shoes.

Quiero zapatos planos.

I want leather-soled shoes.

Quiero zapatos con suela de cuero.

rubber-soled shoes.	suela de goma.
cork-soled shoes.	suela de corcho.

These are not comfortable.

Estos no son cómodos.

May I try the other shoe?

¿Puedo probarme el otro zapato?

Have you got a shoe horn?

¿Tiene un calzador?

They are not my style.

No son de mi estilo.

What other colours have you got?

¿Qué otros colores tiene?

How much are they?

¿Cuánto cuestan?

That is more than I want to pay.

Es más de lo que quiero pagar.

I will wear them. Will you please wrap up my own shoes.

Los llevaré puestos. Puede envolver mis otros zapatos, por favor.

Do you sell shoe polish/shoe cleaner/shoe brushes?

¿Vende crema para zapatos/limpia zapatos/cepillo para zapatos?

Shopping

Tobacconist's

A packet/carton of . . . cigarettes, please.	**Un paquete/cartón de . . . cigarrillos, por favor.**
A box of matches, please.	**Una caja de cerillas, por favor.**
Do you sell English cigarettes?	**¿Vende cigarrillos ingleses?**
What is the local brand?	**¿Cuál es la marca del país?**
Are they Virginia or French/Egyptian/Turkish/American tobacco?	**¿Son de tabaco de Virginia o francés/egipcio/turco/americano?**
Have you any filter tips/king size/menthol cooled?	**¿Tiene emboquillados/largos/mentolados?**
Do you sell pipe tobacco?	**¿Tiene tabaco para pipa?**
May I see your selection of pipes?	**¿Puedo ver su selección de pipas?**
I'd like a cigar.	**Quiero un puro.**
Have you a cigar cutter?	**¿Tiene un cortador de puros?**
Do you sell pipe cleaners?	**¿Vende escobillas?**
I'd like some snuff.	**Quiero rapé.**
Do you have matches?	**¿Tiene cerillas?**

VOCABULARY

box	**la caja**
carton	**el cartón**
cigarette case	**la pitillera**
cigarette lighter	**el encendedor**
flint	**la piedra**

gas	**el gas**
lighter fluid	**la gasolina de encendedor**
matches	**las cerillas**
packet	**el paquete**
pipe	**la pipa**
pipe cleaners	**las escobillas**
pouch	**la tabaquera**

Hardware Stores and Electrical Goods

I'd like a heavy-duty saucepan. a non-stick frying pan.	**Quiero un cazo pesado.** **una sartén que no se pegue.**
Have you a grill/charcoal?	**¿Tiene una parrilla/carbón de leña?**
I need a plastic/metal can for water.	**Necesito un envase de plástico/metal para el agua.**
I'll have a bucket, please.	**Me da un cubo, por favor.**
Have you a ball of strong twine?	**¿Tiene un ovillo de bramante fuerte?**
I need a tow rope and a hook.	**Necesito una soga de remolque y un gancho.**
I need a battery for my torch/radio.	**Necesito una batería para mi linterna/radio.**

VOCABULARY

adapter	**el adaptador**
basket	**el cesto**
battery	**la batería, pila**
brush	**el cepillo**
bulb	**la bombilla**

Shopping

chamois leather	la gamuza
distilled water	el agua destilada
duster	el paño para el polvo, la bayeta
car radio	la radio para coche
fork	el tenedor
hammer	el martillo
insulating tape	la cinta aislante
knife	el cuchillo
mallet	el mazo
penknife	la navaja
percolator	la cafetera de filtro
plug	el enchufe
saw	la sierra
scissors	las tijeras
screwdriver	el atornillador
shaver	la máquina de afeitar
spoons	las cucharas
string	la cuerda
tweezers	las pinzas
wire	el alambre
wrench	la llave inglesa

Chemist's

Do I need a doctor's prescription?	¿Necesito una receta del médico?
Is there an all-night chemist open?	¿Hay una farmacia de guardia?
Can you make up this prescription?	¿Me puede preparar esta receta?
When will it be ready?	¿Cuándo estará lista?
Will you write down the instructions in English if possible?	¿Puede escribir las instrucciones en inglés si es posible?

Is this safe/dangerous for children?	¿Es esto para/ peligroso para niños?
Have you anything for a cold/ sore throat/cough?	¿Tiene algo para el resfriado/ la garganta inflamada/la tos?
I'd like to buy a thermometer.	Necesito un termómetro.
Would you please have a look at this cut/bruise?	Por favor ¿puede mirar este corte/contusión?
What kind of bandage would be best?	¿Qué clase de venda sería mejor?
I've got an upset stomach.	Tengo el estómago transtornado.
diarrhoea.	diarrea.
indigestion.	indigestión.
a headache.	dolor de cabeza.
sunburn.	quemadura de sol.
constipation.	estreñimiento.

VOCABULARY

MEDICINES

aspirin	la aspirina
antibiotic	el antibiótico
bandage	la venda
band-aids	las tiritas, el esparadrapo
corn plasters	los parches para callos
cough lozenges	las pastillas para la tos
cough mixture	el jarabe para la tos
cotton wool	el algodón hidrófilo
disinfectant	el desinfectante
ear drops	las gotas para el oído
gargle	el gargarismo

gauze	la gasa
insect repellent	la loción contra insectos
iodine	el yodo
iron pills	las píldoras de hierro
laxative	el laxativo
lip salve	el cacao para labios
sanitary towels	las compresas
sedative	el calmante
sleeping pill	el somnífero
thermometer	el termómetro
tranquilizers	los sedantes
vitamins	las vitaminas

TOILET ARTICLES

after shave	la loción para después del afeitado
astringent	el astringente
bath oil	el aceite de baño
bath salts	las sales de baño
cologne	la colonia
comb	el peine
cream, cleansing	la crema, limpiadora
cuticle	quitacutículas
foundation	maquillaje
moisturing	hidratante
deodorant	el desodorante
dummy	el chupete
emery board	la lima de papel
eye pencil	el lápiz de ojos
eye shadow	la sombra de ojos
face pack	la crema para mascarilla
face powder	los polvos de la cara
hairbrush	el cepillo para el pelo
hair spray	la laca para el pelo
lipstick	el pintalabios
nailbrush	el cepillo de uñas
nailfile	la lima de uñas
nail polish	el esmalte de uñas

nail polish remover	la acetona, quita-esmalte
nappies	los pañales
perfume	el perfume
plastic pants	las bragas de plástico
rouge	el colorete
safety pins	los imperdibles
setting lotion	el fijador
shampoo	el champú
shaving brush	la brocha de afeitar
shaving cream	la crema de afeitar
soap	el jabón
suntan oil	el aceite bronceador
sponge	la esponja
talcum powder	los polvos de talco
tissues	los pañuelos de papel
toilet paper	el papel del wáter
toothbrush	el cepillo de dientes
toothpaste	la pasta de dientes

At the Photographer's

I'd like to buy a camera.	**Quisiera una máquina fotográfica.**
One that is cheap and easy to use.	**Una que sea barata y sencilla de usar.**
Will you please check my camera?	**Por favor ¿puede inspeccionar mi máquina?**
The film gets stuck.	**La película se atasca.**
The exposure meter is not working.	**El fotómetro no funciona.**
The flash does not light up.	**El magnesio no da luz.**
The film winder is jammed.	**El carrete está atascado.**

Shopping

Can you do it soon?	¿Lo puede hacer pronto?
Will you please process this film?	¿Puede revelar esta película?
I want some black and white/ colour film. colour prints.	Quiero una película en blanco y negro/en color. positivas en color.
Is this film for use in daylight or artificial light?	¿Es esta película para uso con luz del día o luz artificial?
I need a light meter.	Necesito un fotómetro.
How much is an electronic flash?	¿Cuánto es un flash electrónico?

VOCABULARY

films 120, 127, 135, 620	película ciento veinte/ciento veintisiete/ciento treinta y cinco/seiscientos veinte
20 exposures, 36 exposures	veinte exposiciones/treinta y seis exposiciones.
a fast film/a fine-grain film	una película rápida/de grano fino
ciné film 8mm/16mm	película cinematográfica ocho milímetros/dieciséis milímetros
flash bulbs	las bombillas de flash
lens	el objetivo
lens cap	el capuchón para el objetivo
red filter	el filtro rojo
yellow filter	el filtro amarillo
ultra violet	ultravioleta

range finder	**el telémetro**
shutter	**el obturador**
long focus lens	**el objetivo de foco largo**
wide angle lens	**el objetivo de foco ancho**
camera case	**la caja de la máquina**

Bookshop/Stationer's

On which shelf are the books on art/history/politics/sport?
¿En qué estante están los libros de arte/historia/política/deporte?

Where are the guide books?
¿Dónde están los libros de guías?

I want a pocket dictionary.
Necesito un diccionario de bolsillo.

Have you any English newspapers?
¿Tiene periódicos ingleses?

Have you any English paperbacks?
¿Tiene libros en rústica ingleses?

Can you recommend an easy-to-read book in Spanish?
¿Me puede recomendar un libro fácil de leer en español?

Do you sell second-hand books?
¿Vende libros de segunda mano?

I want a map of the area.
Quiero un mapa de la zona.

The scale of this one is too small.
La escala de éste es demasiado pequeña.

Have you got refills for this ballpoint pen?
¿Tiene recambios para este bolígrafo?

Can you please deliver the English newspaper every morning?
Por favor ¿puede enviar el periódico inglés cada mañana?

Shopping

address book	el libro de direcciones
box of crayons	la caja de tizas
carbon paper	el papel carbón
cellophane	el celofán
drawing paper	el papel de dibujo
drawing pins	las chinchetas
envelopes	los sobres
excercise book	el cuaderno
fountain pen	la pluma estilográfica
greaseproof paper	el papel apergaminado
glue	la cola
ink	la tinta
label	la etiqueta
notebook	el libro de notas
notepaper	el papel para cartas
paste	el engrudo
pen	la pluma
pencil	el lapicero
pencil sharpener	el sacaminas
playing cards	la baraja
postcards	las tarjetas
rubber	la goma de borrar
ruler	la regla
Sellotape	la cinta adhesiva
silver foil	el papel de plata
tissue paper	el papel de seda
typewriter ribbon	la cinta para máquina
typing paper	el papel de máquina
writing pad	el block de papel

Buying Souvenirs

Are all these things made in Spain?	¿Están todas estas cosas hechas en España?
This is a nice straw hat.	Este es un sombrero de paja bonito.
I like this bag.	Esta bolsa me gusta.
Have you any costume jewellery?	¿Tiene joyas de fantasía?
I'm looking for bracelet charms.	Estoy buscando dijes para el brazalete.
I'd like to try on that ring.	Me gustaría probarme ese anillo.
What is this bracelet made of?	¿De qué está hecho este brazalete?
I'd like some local pottery.	Quisiera cerámica regional.
Can you pack this carefully?	¿Puede enpaquetar esto con cuidado?
Do you despatch things abroad?	¿Envían cosas al extranjero?
I'm just looking around.	Sólo estoy mirando.
I will come back later.	Volveré más tarde.
Can I leave a deposit on it and return tomorrow?	¿Puedo dejar una fianza y volver mañana?
Do you take foreign cheques with a Eurocard?	¿Aceptan cheques extranjeros con una Eurocard?

Shopping

Vocabulary

beads	**el abalorio**
brooch	**el broche**
chain	**la cadena**
cigarette lighter	**el encendedor**
clock	**el reloj**
cuff links	**los gemelos**
earrings	**los pendientes**
jewel box	**el joyero**
music box	**la caja musical**
necklace	**el collar**
ring	**el anillo**
rosary	**el rosario**
silverware	**los objetos de plata**
watch	**el reloj**
watchstrap	**la correa de reloj**
wristwatch	**el reloj de pulsera**

Entertainment

Out for the Evening
Nightclubs

Can you recommend a nightclub with a good show?	¿Puede recomendar un club de noche con un buen espectáculo?
a place with dancing and cabaret?	un lugar para bailar con cabaret?
a disco?	una discoteca?
an open-air dance?	un baile al aire libre?
a nightclub with hostesses?	un club de noche con cabareteras?
Is there an entrance fee?	¿Hay una cuota de entrada?
Does it include drinks?	¿Incluye bebidas?
What is the cost of drinks?	¿Cuál es el coste de las bebidas?
At what time does the show start?	¿A qué hora empieza el espectáculo?
Is there a different price for drinks at the bar?	¿Hay un precio diferente para las bebidas en el mostrador?
I do not want a photograph.	No quiero una foto.
May I have this dance?	¿Me permite este baile?

Cinemas

What is on at the cinema?	¿Qué ponen en el cine?
Have you got a guide to what's on?	¿Tiene una cartelera de espectáculos?

Entertainment

Two stalls, please.	**Dos butacas, por favor.**
At what time does it start?	**¿A qué hora empieza?**
Will we have to queue for long?	**¿Tendremos que hacer fila por mucho tiempo?**
I want a seat near the front/at the back/in the middle.	**Quiero un asiento cerca de la delantera/en la parte de atrás/hacia en medio.**
Do I tip the usherette?	**¿Le doy propina a la acomodadora?**
I'd rather sit over there.	**Preferiría sentarme por allí.**
Will you please shine your torch here?	**Por favor ¿puede enfocar su antorcha aquí?**
I have dropped something.	**Se me ha caído algo.**
Is there an icecream seller?	**¿Hay un vendedor de helados?**
At what time does the main film start?	**¿A qué hora empieza la película principal?**
Will you please move over to the right/left?	**Por favor, ¿puede moverse hacia la derecha/izquierda?**
Remove your hat, please.	**Quítese el sombrero, por favor.**

VOCABULARY

actor	**el actor**
actress	**la actriz**
director	**el director**
dubbing	**el doblaje**
interval	**el intérvalo**
producer	**el productor**

projector	**el proyector**
screen	**la pantalla**
sound	**el sonido**
star	**la estrella**

Theatre/Opera

Is there a ticket agency near?	**¿Hay una agencia de entradas cerca?**
Is there another way of getting a ticket?	**¿Hay otro modo de obtener una entrada?**
Are there any last-minute returns?	**¿Hay devoluciones en el último momento?**
Do we have to wear evening dress?	**¿Tenemos que llevar traje de noche?**
I'd like a souvenir programme.	**Quisiera un programa de recuerdo.**
What is the name of the prima donna?	**¿Cuál es el nombre de la diva?**
Who is the leading actor?	**¿Quién es el actor principal?**
How long is the interval?	**¿Cuánto dura el descanso?**
Where is the bar?	**¿Dónde está el bar?**

VOCABULARY

applause	**el aplauso**
audience	**el auditorio**
baritone	**el barítono**
bass	**el bajo**
composer	**el compositor**

Entertainment

conductor	el director
contralto	la contralto
encore	la repetición
orchestra	la orquesta
playwright	el dramaturgo
scenery	el decorado
soprano	la soprano
stage	el escenario
tenor	el tenor

Concert Hall

I want a seat from which I can see the pianist's hands.	**Quiero un asiento desde donde pueda ver las manos del/de la pianista.**
Can I buy the score?	**¿Puedo comprar la partitura?**
Who is conducting tonight?	**¿Quién dirige esta noche?**
Who is the soloist?	**¿Quién es el/la soloista?**

VOCABULARY

bass	el bajo
bassoon	el bajón
brass	el cobre
cello	el violoncelo
clarinet	el clarinete
cymbals	los platillos
drum	el tambor
flute	la flauta
French horn	el corno de caza
percussion	los instrumentos de percusión
saxophone	el saxofón

strings	**los instrumentos de cuerda**
timpani	**los tímpanos**
trombone	**el trombón**
trumpet	**la trompeta**
violin	**el violín**
wind	**los instrumentos de viento**

Casino

What games are played here?	**¿A qué se juega aquí?**
What is the minimum stake in this room?	**¿Cuál es la mínima puesta en esta sala?**
Can I buy some chips?	**¿Puedo comprar fichas?**
I should like 5,000 pesetas worth.	**Quisiera el valor de cinco mil pesetas.**
Excuse me, those are my chips.	**Perdone, esas son mis fichas.**
Where can I cash my chips?	**¿Dónde puedo cobrar mis fichas?**
I'm bust.	**Estoy arruinado.**
I'll take another card.	**Deme otra carta.**
No more.	**Nada más.**
Pass me the dice please.	**Páseme los dados, por favor.**

VOCABULARY

ace	**el as**
bet	**la apuesta**
blackjack	**veintiuno**
cards	**las cartas**
chemin de fer	**chemin de fer**

107

On the Beach

clubs	los tréboles
croupier	el crupier
diamonds	los diamantes
hearts	los corazones
jack	la sota
joker	el comodín
king	el rey
poker	póker
queen	la dama
spades	los picos, las espadas

| Faites vos jeux | Hagan juego |
| Rien ne va plus | No va más |

Out for the Day
On the Beach

Does one have to pay to use this beach?	¿Se paga en esta playa?
Is there a free section of the beach?	¿Hay un área libre en la playa?
Is it clean?	¿Está limpia?
How much does it cost per day/per week to hire a cabin?	¿Cuánto cuesta por día/por semana alquilar una cabina?
deckchairs?	las sillas de lona?
air mattress?	un colchón neumático?
sun umbrella?	una sombrilla?
Can I leave valuables in the cabin?	¿Puedo dejar objetos de valor en la cabina?
Is the ticket valid all day?	¿Sirve la entrada para todo el día?
Does the beach shelve steeply?	¿Está el fondo en fuerte declive?

Is it safe for swimming?	¿Se puede nadar sin peligro?
Are there any currents?	¿Hay corrientes?
Is it safe to dive off the rocks?	¿Se puede bucear desde las rocas sin peligro?
Where is the freshwater shower?	¿Dónde está la ducha de agua corriente?
Have you any tar remover?	¿Tiene algo para quitar la brea?
Can I hire a swimsuit?	¿Puedo alquilar un traje de baño?
I've cut my foot. Have you any elastoplast?	Me he cortado el pie. ¿Tiene esparadrapo?
Do you keep lost property?	¿Guarda objetos perdidos?
Is there a children's beach club?	¿Hay un club de playa para niños?
At what time are the keep fit classes?	¿A qué hora son las clases para mantenerse en forma?
Is there water-ski tuition available?	¿Hay enseñanza de esquí acuático?
Does it matter if I can't swim?	¿Importa si no se nadar?
Where is the nearest beach shop?	¿Dónde está la tienda más cercana de la playa?
Have you got a life jacket?	¿Tiene un chaleco salvavidas?
Is this a good place for skin diving?	¿Es este un buen sitio para la natación submarina?
Help! I'm in difficulty!	¡Socorro! ¡Me encuentro sin fuerza!

VOCABULARY

beach ball	la pelota de playa
cactus	el cacto
goggles	las gafas submarinas
harpoon gun	la pistola de arpón
high tide	la marea alta
lilo	el colchón neumático
low tide	la marea baja
net	la red
pedalo	el pedalo
pines	los pinos
promenade	el paseo
raft	la balsa
rocks	las rocas
rowing boat	la barca de remo
sand	la arena
sandals	las sandalias
sea	el mar
seaweed	las algas
shells	las conchas
shingle	el guijarro
sun oil	el aceite para el sol
surf	la ola
surf board	la plancha de deslizamiento
underwater	submarina
waterski instructor	el instructor de esquí acuático
yacht	el yate

Sightseeing

Where can I get a good guide book?	¿Dónde puedo encontrar una buena guía?
Is there an excursion round the city?	¿Hay una excursión de la ciudad?

Is it a conducted party?	**¿Hay un grupo con guía?**
Am I allowed to go round alone?	**¿Puedo dar una vuelta solo?**
Where do I find an official guide?	**¿Dónde hay un guía oficial?**
Does the whole-day excursion include lunch?	**¿Está la comida incluida en la excursión para todo el día?**
Are the entrance fees extra?	**¿Son extra las entradas?**
Should I tip the guide/driver?	**¿Debo dar una propina al guía/conductor?**
I'd like to stay here longer.	**Quisiera quedarme un poco más.**
I'll meet the party later.	**Me uniré más tarde al grupo.**
Where will you be?	**¿Dónde estará?**
Will you please write it down?	**¿Lo puede escribir, por favor?**
Can I hire an audioguide?	**¿Puedo alquilar un audioguía?**

In Churches

Do ladies have to cover their heads?	**¿Se deben de cubrir la cabeza las señoras?**
Is it all right to enter like this?	**¿Está bien entrar así?**
How old is this church?	**¿Es muy antigua esta iglesia?**
Who founded it?	**¿Quién la fundó?**
Are the stained glass windows original?	**¿Son estas vidrieras de colores las originales?**
Can one illuminate the fresco?	**¿Se puede iluminar el fresco?**

Sightseeing

Is one allowed to go up the bell tower?	**¿Está permitido subir al campanario?**
Is there a book about the church?	**¿Hay un libro acerca de la iglesia?**
May I leave a small contribution?	**¿Puedo dejar una pequeña contribución?**

VOCABULARY

abbey	**la abadía**
aisles	**las naves**
altar	**el altar**
arch	**el arco**
candle	**la vela**
cathedral	**la catedral**
chapel	**la capilla**
cloister	**el claustro**
crucifix	**el crucifijo**
crypt	**la cripta**
choir	**el coro**
column	**la columna**
convent	**el convento**
fresco	**el fresco**
font	**la pila**
monastery	**el monasterio**
nave	**la nave**
rood	**la cruz**
sculpture	**la escultura**
shrine	**el santuario**

Art Galleries and Museums

Have you a catalogue/illustrated catalogue?	**¿Tiene un catálogo/catálogo ilustrado?**

Are there any plaster casts?	**¿Hay vaciados?**
Do you sell transparencies?	**¿Vende diapositivas?**
Am I allowed to photograph?	**¿Puedo sacar fotografías?**
May I use my tripod?	**¿Puedo usar el trípode?**
Is the gallery open on Sundays?	**¿Está la galería abierta los domingos?**
Is it free?	**¿Es gratis?**
Where can I find the Dutch School?	**¿Dónde está la escuela flamenca?**
Do you make photocopies?	**¿Hace fotocopias?**
Where is the library?	**¿Dónde está la biblioteca?**

VOCABULARY

antique books	**los libros antiguos**
bas relief	**el bajorelieve**
china	**la porcelana**
costumes	**los vestidos**
drawing	**el dibujo**
engraving	**el grabado**
etching	**el aguafuerte**
frame	**el marco**
furniture	**los muebles**
jewellery	**las joyas**
lithograph	**la litografía**
miniature	**la miniatura**
porcelain	**la porcelana**
pottery	**la cerámica**
silverware	**la plata**

Historical Sights

Will there be far to walk?	¿Hay que andar mucho?
Can I wait here till you return?	¿Puedo esperar aquí hasta que vuelva?
Is there a souvenir stall?	¿Hay un puesto de recuerdos?
Where can we get a cold drink?	¿Dónde hay bebidas frescas?
Is there a plan of the grounds?	¿Hay un plano de los jardines?
I would like to walk round the gardens.	Me gustaría pasear por los jardines.

Vocabulary

amphitheatre	el anfiteatro
aquaduct	el acueducto
arena	la arena
armour	la armadura
battlements	las almenas
cannon	el cañón
catacombs	las catacumbas
castle	el castillo
column	la columna
courtyard	el patio
crossbow	la ballesta
fort	el fuerte
fortifications	las fortificaciones
forum	el foro
fountain	la fuente
gate	la puerta
pediment	el frontón
portcullis	el rastrillo

viaduct	el viaducto
wall	el muro

Gardens

Are these gardens open to the public?	¿Están abiertos al público los jardines?
Can we walk where we like?	¿Puedo andar por donde quiera?
How long will it take to walk round?	¿Cuánto llevará dar una vuelta?
At what time do you close?	¿A qué hora cierran?
Is there a plan of the gardens?	¿Hay un plano de los jardines?
Where is the greenhouse/tropical plant house?	¿Dónde está el invernadero/el pabellón de las plantas tropicales?
May we sit on the grass?	¿Nos podemos sentar en la hierba?
What is the name of that plant/flower?	¿Cómo se llama esa planta/flor?
Is there a lake/pond?	¿Hay un lago/estanque?
Who designed these gardens?	¿Quién planeó estos jardines?

VOCABULARY

ash	el fresno
beech	la haya
birch	el abedul

Sightseeing

bougainvillea	**la buganvilla**
carnation	**el clavel**
cherry tree	**el cerezo**
chrysanthemum	**el crisántemo**
clematis	**el clemátide**
daffodil	**el narciso**
dahlia	**la dalia**
daisy	**la margarita**
deciduous trees	**los árboles de hoja caduca**
elm	**el olmo**
evergreen	**el árbol de hoja perenne**
fir	**el abeto**
geranium	**el geranio**
herbaceous border	**el borde herbáceo**
ivy	**la yedra**
lily	**la azucena**
moss	**el musgo**
nasturtium	**la capuchina**
oak	**el roble**
pear tree	**el peral**
pine	**el pino**
plane	**el plátano**
poplar	**el chopo**
rose	**la rosa**
tulip	**el tulipán**
violet	**la violeta**
wisteria	**la vistaria**

The Zoo

The children would like to visit the zoo.	**Los niños quisieran ver el zoo.**
Is it open every day?	**¿Está abierto todos los días?**
Is there a nature reserve?	**¿Hay una reserva natural?**

Can one drive through it?	¿Se puede conducir a través?
Where can we park the car?	¿Dónde podemos aparcar el coche?
Where can one buy animal food?	¿Dónde se puede comprar comida para los animales?
When is feeding time?	¿A qué hora se les da de comer?
Is there an insect house?	¿Hay un pabellón de insectos?
Can the children ride an elephant?	¿Se pueden montar los niños en el elefante?
Is there a children's zoo?	¿Hay un zoo para niños?

VOCABULARY

antelope	el antilope
ants	las hormigas
aquarium	el acuario
baboon	el mandril
bat	el murciélago
bird	el pájaro
bison	el bisonte
cat	el gato
crocodile	el cocodrilo
dog	el perro
frog	la rana
giraffe	la jirafa
hippopotamus	el hipopótamo
horse	el caballo
hyena	la hiena
leopard	el leopardo
lion	el león

Sightseeing

parrot	**el papagayo**
rhinoceros	**el rinoceronte**
seal	**la foca**
snake	**la culebra**
turtle	**la tortuga**
zebra	**la zebra**

Sport

Spanish-speaking people follow football, bicycle racing and athletics with the same enthusiasm as most of the rest of the world, but they also have sports which are uniquely their own. One of these, if it can be called a sport, is the bullfight and the other is **pelota**, a Basque game.

La Corrida

The bullfight is called **la corrida**, which means, literally, running the bulls, and few people can keep calm when discussing this entertainment. In Spain and Mexico where the bullfight has a loyal following, bullfighters have the same status as film stars and are forgotten as quickly if they fail to give the public what it wants.

The bullfight is a highly formal encounter between man and beast. It begins with the running of the bull by the various matadors, each of whom makes the bull charge at his cape. This indicates to the matador who will have to kill it what the bull's characteristics are, for example, whether it hooks to the right or left, turns fast, and so on.

The second stage, announced by the sounding of trumpets, introduces the picador, a Quixote-like figure on horseback whose role is to withstand the bull's charge with a lance which damages the bull's neck muscles and therefore makes him less powerful, though not less dangerous.

The third stage is the placing of the banderillas, two sets of decorated darts, between the bull's shoulder blades. This is accomplished by a man without a cape whose only defence against the charging beast is his own agility and speed.

The final stage is the duel between the matador and the bull. The matador plays the bull with a smaller cape, the muleta, in which he carries the sword with which he will despatch the

animal. The object of this section of the **corrida** is to show
the matador's skill at dominating the bull and preparing him
for the moment when he will stand in the correct way to make
a kill possible. Matadors who are trying to make their
reputation, or who already have a big name to maintain, often
take extraordinary risks and this provides the excitement that
the crowd seeks.

The kill should be accomplished by one clean thrust, but
unfortunately this is rarely achieved. After repeated failures,
the bull is despatched by a short dagger thrust in the back of
the neck. Bullfighters who have done well are rewarded by the
presentation of the animal's ears and tail. These often end up
in the lap of the person to whom the matador has dedicated
the bull.

Bullfights start at five o'clock in the afternoon when the sun is
low and for this reason the best seats are those with their
backs to the sun, **sombra**. These are the most expensive and
the nearer they are to the arena the more pricey they become.
Sol y sombra means a seat which will be in the sun for part
of the **corrida** and in the shade for the latter half. A seat in
sol will face the sun for most of the bullfight. Bullring seats
are very hard and cushions are hired out by itinerant vendors.
Other vendors will sell icecream, programmes, hats and even
brandy for those who find the **corrida** more than they
bargained for.

I would like to go to a bullfight.	**Quisiera ir a una corrida.**
Where is the bullring?	**¿Dónde está la plaza de toros?**
Have you got a seat in the shade/sun/open/amphitheatre/first row?	**¿Tiene asiento de sombra/sol/tendido/grada/barrera?**
How much is it?	**¿Cuánto es?**
Where is our seat?	**¿Dónde está nuestro asiento?**

What is the bullfighter's name?	**¿Como se llama el torero?**
Is he good?	**¿Es bueno?**
How many bulls will he fight?	**¿Cuántos toros tiene que lidiar?**
Can I rent a cushion?	**¿Puedo alquilar una almohadilla?**

VOCABULARY

amphitheatre	**la grada**
bull	**el toro**
bullfight	**la corrida**
bullfighter	**el torero**
bullfighter's cape and stick	**la muleta**
bullfighter's costume	**el traje de luces**
bullfighter on horse	**el picador**
bullring	**la plaza de toros**
cloak	**el capote**
dart	**la banderilla**
ear	**la oreja**
hat	**la montera**
horn	**el cuerno**
legs	**las patas**
man who sticks the darts	**el banderillero**
ring	**la arena, el ruedo**
sword	**la espada**
tail	**el rabo**
team	**la cuadrilla**
uncovered seat	**el tendido**
walk round the ring	**la vuelta al ruedo**

Sport

Pelota

The word **pelota** literally translated means ball. **Pelota** is played by two teams in a court called a **frontón**. Players wear a long, curved wicker basket, called the **cesta**, on their hand. The ball is hard and covered in leather. The player swings the ball along the basket and serves it against the end wall. The ball travels very fast and it is the job of the opposing player to catch and return it.

Spectators sit along one side of the court, protected by wire, and may place bets with a bookie who shouts the odds at the crowd, takes money, issues betting tickets and somehow keeps the whole thing going throughout the game until the end when he pays out to lucky punters.

This is an entertainment that few visitors attend, but one that should not be missed for its local colour and excitement without bloodshed. In Latin America a version of **pelota** is played called **jai-alai**.

Football

Where is the stadium?	**¿Dónde está el estadio?**
How does one get there?	**¿Cómo se va allí?**
Should I book tickets?	**¿Tengo que reservar entradas?**
Will it be very crowded?	**¿Estará muy lleno?**
Who is playing?	**¿Quienes juegan?**
Is there a local team?	**¿Hay un equipo local?**
I want a ticket for the main stand/a place under cover/in the open.	**Quiero una entrada de tribuna/bajo cubierta/al descubierto.**
May I have a programme?	**¿Me da un programa?**

Vocabulary

area	área
attack	el ataque
defence	la defensa
football	el fútbol
goalkeeper	el portero
goal posts	los postes
halfway line	la línea media
penalty area	la area de penálty
players	los jugadores
referee	el árbitro
score	el tanteo
team	el equipo

Race Meetings

I want a ticket for the paddock/a grandstand seat, please.	Quiero una entrada para la explanada de ensillado/un asiento de tribuna, por favor.
Where can I place a bet?	¿Dónde puedo hacer una apuesta?
What are the odds on number 5?	¿Qué son los puntos de ventaja en el número cinco?
I'd like to back it to win/each way/for a place.	Apostaré a ganar el primer puesto/ganador y colocado/para colocado.
Which is the favourite?	¿Cuál es el favorito?
I will back the outsider.	Apostaré en el que no es favorito.
Is the jockey well known?	¿Es bien conocido el jockey?

Sport

course	la pista
filly	la potra
flat-race	la carrera en liso
horse	el caballo
hurdles	las vallas
jockey	el jockey
owner	el dueño
photo finish	el resultado comprobado por fotocontrol
rails	la cerca
stable	la cuadra
starting gate	la barrera de salida
tote	el totalizador
trainer	el preparador

Tennis

Is there a tennis club near here?	¿Hay un club de tenis por aquí?
Where is the championship being held?	¿Dónde tienen lugar los campeonatos?
How can I get some tickets?	¿Cómo puedo obtener entradas?
Should I arrive early?	¿Debo de llegar pronto?
Who is playing?	¿Quién juega?
Is it on hard courts or grass?	¿Es sobre pista dura o de hierba?
I want to watch the men's singles/doubles/mixed doubles.	Quiero ver las partidas individuales de hombres/la partida doble/la partida mixta.

How do you score in Spanish?	¿Cómo se puntúa en español?
15, 30, 40, deuce, advantage in/out, game, set, match.	Quince, treinta, cuarenta, a dos, ventaja del saque/del que recibe, juego, set, partida.
Shall we toss for service?	¿Echamos para el saque?
Let's adjust the net.	Ajustemos la red.
It's too high/too low.	Está demasiado alta/demasiado baja.
That was out/in/on the line.	Estaba fuera/dentro/en la línea.
Good shot.	Buena tirada.
Will you keep the score?	¿Puede llevar el tanteo?
Change ends.	Cambien de lado.

VOCABULARY

backhand	el revés
forehand	el derecho
racquet	la raqueta
rally	el peloteo
smash	el smash
spin	el giro de la pelota
tennis ball	la pelota de tenis
umpire	el árbitro
volley	la volea

Sport

Golf

Is there a golf course nearby?	¿Hay un campo de golf por aquí?
Does one have to be a member?	¿Tiene uno que ser miembro?
Is there temporary membership?	¿Se puede ser socio temporalmente?
How much does it cost to play?	¿Cuánto cuesta jugar?
I'd like a caddie.	Quisiera un cadi.
Are there any trolleys for hire?	¿Hay carretillas para alquilar?
I'd like to speak to the professional.	Quisiera hablar con el profesional.
Are you free for lessons?	¿Está libre para dar lecciones?
Will you play a round with me?	¿Quiere jugar una vuelta conmigo?
My handicap is eighteen.	Mi desventaja es dieciocho.
I can't get any length on my drive.	No puedo tirar el golpe de salida muy lejos.
My approach shots are weak.	Mis tiros de cerca son débiles.
I'll do some putting while I wait for you.	Tiraré al hoyo mientras le espero.
Can I hire some clubs?	¿Puedo alquilar palos?
May I have a scorecard?	¿Me da una tarjeta de tanteo?

VOCABULARY

---

bunker	**la hoya de arena**
club house	**el edificio del club**
fairway	**el recorrido**
golf bag	**el saco de golf**
green	**el césped**
irons	**el acero**
mashie	**el palo de cabeza curba**
niblick	**una clase de palo**
par	**el mínimo de jugadas**
rough	**el terreno quebrado**
tee	**el tee, la salida**
to slice	**cortar**

Water-skiing

I have never skied before. Not even on snow.	**No he esquiado nunca. Ni en la nieve.**
I am not a good swimmer.	**No soy buen nadador.**
Do I wear a life jacket?	**¿Me pongo un chaleco salvavidas?**
Will you please help me to put on the skis?	**¿Me puede ayudar a ponerme los esquís?**
Please pass me the rope.	**Me pase la cuerda, por favor.**
May I ride on the speed boat?	**¿Puedo ir en la lancha?**
Can I borrow a wetsuit?	**¿Me puede prestar un traje de goma?**
I'm ready now.	**Estoy listo.**
Just a moment.	**Un momento.**

Sport

aquaplane	el hidroavión
bathing hat	el gorro de goma
goggles	las gafas submarinas
jump	el salto

Riding

Is there a riding stable at the resort?	¿Hay una caballeriza con caballos de montar aquí?
Can I hire a horse for riding?	¿Puedo alquilar un caballo para montar?
Do you give lessons?	¿Da lecciones?
I'd like to go on a ride.	Quisiera dar un paseo a caballo.
I want a quiet horse.	Quiero un caballo manso.
Have you any ponies?	¿Tiene poneys?
Will an instructor accompany the ride?	¿Habrá un instructor durante el recorrido?
I'd like to practise jumping.	Quisiera practicar el salto.
I am an experienced rider/a novice.	Soy un jinete con experiencia/novato.
Do you have English saddles?	¿Tiene sillas inglesas?
This horse has gone lame.	Este caballo cojea.
The girth is too loose.	La cincha esta floja.
Will you please adjust my stirrups?	¿Puede ajustar mis estribos?

Will you hold my horse while I get on?	**¿Puede agarrar mi caballo mientras monto?**
Will you give me a leg-up?	**¿Me ayuda a subir?**

VOCABULARY

bit	**el freno**
blinkers	**las anteojeras**
bridle	**la brida**
girth	**la cincha**
harness	**los arreos**
hock	**el corvejón**
hoof	**el casco**
mare	**la yegua**
martingale	**la amarra**
reins	**las riendas**
stallion	**el garañon**
withers	**la cruz**

Fishing

Where can I get a permit to fish?	**¿Dónde puedo obtener una licencia para pescar?**
Are there places for fishing in this area?	**¿Hay sitios para pescar en este área?**
Are there any trout or salmon?	**¿Hay trucha o salmón?**
How much does a day's fishing cost?	**¿Cuánto cuesta pescar por un día?**
Is that per rod?	**¿Es eso por caña?**
Where can I get some bait?	**¿Dónde puedo encontrar cebo?**

Sport

What is the minimum size that I am allowed to keep?	**¿Cuál es el tamaño mínimo que se permite guardar?**
What is the best time of day to go out?	**¿Cuál es la mejor hora del día para salir?**
Are there any boats that will take me deep sea fishing?	**¿Hay alguna embarcación que me pueda llevar a la pesca de altura?**
Do they provide tackle?	**¿Proveen los aparejos?**

VOCABULARY

fishing season	**la temporada de pesca**
fly	**la mosca**
float	**el corcho**
gaff	**el arpón**
hook	**el anzuelo**
line	**el sedal**
lure	**el cebo**
net	**la red**
reel	**el carrete**
spinner	**la cuchara/el cebo**
weights	**el lastre**

Shooting

Where can I shoot?	**¿Dónde puedo cazar?**
Do I need a licence?	**¿Necesito una licencia?**
I'd like to borrow a 12-bore shotgun.	**Quisiera que me prestasen una escopeta de calibre doce.**
I have my own rifle.	**Tengo mi propio rifle.**

Is there a shooting party I could join?	¿Hay alguna partida de caza a la que me pueda agregar?
Is there a clay pigeon shoot?	¿Hay tiro al pichón?
Is there a rifle range near?	¿Hay un campo de tiro cerca?

Vocabulary

backsight	la mira de delante
barrel	el cañon
bullets	las balas
butt	la culata
cartridges	los cartuchos
catch	el pestillo
ejector	el expulsor
foresight	la mira de atrás
hammer	el percusor
revolver	el revólver
safety catch	el seguro
telescopic sight	la mira telescópica
trigger	el gatillo

Sailing and Boating

I'd like to hire a dinghy.	Quisiera alquilar un bote.
Is an outboard motor extra?	¿Es un motor fuera de borda extra?
Does this have an auxiliary engine?	¿Tiene este un motor auxiliar?
How many berths are there?	¿Cuántas literas hay?
How much water does it draw?	¿Cuánto tiene de calado?

Sport

Is there a stove/sink/chemical toilet?	¿Hay un hornillo/una fregadera/un wáter químico?
Are all cutlery, china and cooking utensils included?	¿Están los cubiertos, vajilla y utensilios de cocina incluídos?
Are sheets and blankets provided?	¿Hay provisión de sábanas y mantas?
Have you got a map of the river?	¿Tiene un mapa del río?
Are there many locks to negotiate?	¿Hay que pasar muchas esclusas?
At what time do the locks close?	¿A qué hora cierran las esclusas?
How far is it to the next place where I can get fuel?	¿Cuánta distancia hay hasta el próximo sitio donde puedo obtener combustible?
Can I leave the boat here while we go to the shops?	¿Puedo dejar aquí el barco mientras vamos de compras?
Where is the next refuse dump?	¿Dónde está el próximo vertedero?
Will you please give me a tow?	¿Me puede remolcar?

VOCABULARY

anchor	el ancla
boat	el barco
boathook	el bichero
bow	la proa
canoe	la canoa
chart	la carta de navegación

deck	**la cubierta**
diesel engine	**el motor diesel**
halyards	**las drizas**
hull	**el casco**
jib	**el foque**
keel	**la quilla**
lifebelt	**el cinturón salvavidas**
lifejacket	**el chaleco salvavidas**
mainsail	**la vela mayor**
mast	**el mástil**
motorboat	**la barca motora**
oar	**el remo**
paddle	**el canalete**
pennant	**el gallardete**
port (left)	**el babor**
propeller	**la hélice**
rowing boat	**la barca de remo**
sail	**la vela**
sheet	**la escota**
starboard (right)	**el estribor**
steer	**gobernar**
stern	**la popa**
tiller	**la caña del timón**
yacht	**el yate**

Winter Sports

In the past few years, Spain has developed a number of ski resorts in the Pyrenees and in the Sierra Nevada of Andalusia. Those in the south provide the unusual possibility of dividing a holiday between the snow-clad Sierras and the winter sunshine resorts of the Costa del Sol. The Spanish ski resorts cannot compare with those of established winter sports countries and consist mostly of single hotels or complexes with an adequate, but limited, number of ski lifts.

I'd like to join a class for beginners/intermediate skiers.	Quisiera unirme a un grupo de principiantes/esquiadores intermedios.
Is there a beginner's slope?	¿Hay una ladera para principiantes?
Where can I hire skis?	¿Dónde puedo alquilar esquís?
a toboggan?	un tobogán?
boots?	botas?
ski sticks?	bastones de esquiar?
I have never skied before.	No he esquiado nunca.
These boots are uncomfortable.	Estas botas son incómodas.
They are too tight/loose/big/small.	Me están prietas/anchas/grandes/pequeñas.
How far is the ski hoist from the hotel?	¿A cuánto está el montacargas de esquiar del hotel?
Can I get a season ticket?	¿Puedo obtener un abono?
Are the skiing conditions good this morning?	¿Son buenas las condiciones de esquiar esta mañana?
Are all the pistes open?	¿Están abiertas todas las pistas?
Is there any cross-country skiing?	¿Hay esquí a campo traviesa?
Please help me.	Por favor, me puede ayudar.
I think I've twisted my ankle.	Creo que me he torcido un tobillo.
Two entrance tickets for the ice rink.	Dos entradas para la pista de patinaje.

| Is there a heated swimming pool? | ¿Hay piscina cubierta? |
| Look out! I can't stop! | ¡Cuidado! ¡No puedo parar! |

VOCABULARY

anorak	el anorak
avalanche	la avalancha
cable car	el teleférico
funicular	el funicular
ice	el hielo
ice skating	el patinaje sobre hielo
skates	los patines
ski-lift	el teleskí
slalom	el slalom
snow	la nieve
stem	la vuelta
toboggan run	la pista de tobogán
waterproof trousers	los pantalones impermeables

General Services

If you are travelling independently or having a self-catering holiday at a villa or apartment, phrases for dealing with gas, electricity and plumbing problems will be indispensable. But even when all that is taken care of by someone else, it is useful to be able to communicate with Post Office staff, telephone operators and other officials in their own language.

Post Office

Post Offices in Spain have the sign **Correo y Telégrafos**. You can also buy stamps at a tobacconist.

Where is the nearest Post Office?	**¿Dónde está Correos?**
What are the opening hours?	**¿Qué horas abren?**
Can I cash an international money order here?	**¿Puedo cobrar aquí un giro internacional?**
I want some stamps for a letter to Britain.	**Quiero sellos para una carta a Inglaterra.**
What is the postcard postage rate for the USA?	**¿Cuál es el franqueo de una tarjeta a los Estados Unidos?**
I'd like to register this letter.	**Quisiera certificar esta carta.**
I want to send it airmail. express. by surface. printed matter rate.	**Quiero enviarlo por avión. urgente. por correo ordinario. como impresos.**
Where do I post parcels?	**¿Dónde puedo mandar paquetes por correo?**
Do I need a customs form?	**¿Necesito un impreso de aduana?**

Is there a poste restante here?	¿Hay una lista de correos aquí?
Have you a letter for me?	¿Tiene una carta para mí?
May I have a telegram form?	¿Me da un impreso de telegrama?
I'll send it by the cheap rate/ normal rate.	Lo enviaré por correo ordinario/por avión.
When will it arrive?	¿Cuándo llegará?
I want to make a local telephone call. an international call. a person-to-person call.	Quiero hacer una llamada telefónica local. internacional. de persona a persona.
Can you reverse the charges?	¿Puede cobrar al número llamado?
Switchboard, the line is engaged. Please try again later.	Señorita, el número está comunicando. Por favor, llame más tarde.

The Police Station

I am a visitor to your country.	Estoy visitando su país.
I would like to report a theft/loss/ accident/crime.	Quisiera reportar un robo/ una pérdida/un accidente/un crimen.
Someone stole my wallet.	Alguien me ha robado la cartera.
Something was stolen from my car/hotel room.	Han robado en mi coche/en mi habitación del hotel.
The theft occurred in the Avenida España at about four o'clock.	El robo ocurrió en la Avenida España a eso de las cuatro de la tarde.

I have lost my watch on the beach.	**He perdido mi reloj en la playa.**
It is valuable.	**Es de valor.**
It has sentimental value.	**Tiene valor sentimental.**
I will offer a reward.	**Ofreceré recompensa.**
Someone has been knocked down.	**Alguien ha sido atropellado.**
A lady has broken her leg.	**Una señora se ha roto la pierna.**
There is a man molesting women on the promenade.	**Hay un hombre molestando mujeres por el paseo.**
I have been swindled.	**Me han estafado.**
Can a police officer come with me?	**¿Puede venir un policía conmigo?**
I will be a witness.	**Haré de testigo.**
I cannot be a witness. I did not see what was happening.	**No puedo hacer de testigo. No vi lo que ocurrió.**
Is there anyone who speaks English?	**¿Hay alguien que hable inglés?**

Electricity

The lights have gone out.	Se han apagado las luces.
The power plug is not working.	El enchufe eléctrico no funciona.
The fuse has gone.	El plomo se ha fundido.
I think it's the switch.	Creo que es el interruptor.
There is a smell of burning.	Huele a quemado.
The stove won't light.	El hornillo no se enciende.

The heating has broken down.	**La calefacción no funciona.**
Can you mend it straight away?	**¿Puede arreglarla inmediatamente?**
Where is the fuse box?	**¿Dónde está la caja de fusibles?**
Which is the main switch?	**¿Cuál es el enchufe principal?**

VOCABULARY

adaptor	**el adaptador**
bulb	**la bombilla**
cooker	**la cocina**
electric fire	**el fuego eléctrico**
extension lead	**el cable de extensión**
fuse wire	**el plomo**
hairdryer	**el secador de pelo**
insulating tape	**la cinta aislante**
iron	**la plancha**
plug	**el enchufe**
radio	**la radio**
razor point	**el enchufe para la maquinilla**
refrigerator	**la nevera/el frigorífico**
spotlight	**la luz de foco**
television	**la televisión**
torch	**la linterna**
water heater	**el calentador de agua**

Gas

There is a smell of gas.	**Huele a gas.**
It must be a gas leak.	**Debe de ser un escape de gas.**

General Services

The gas jet won't light.	**El caño de salida no se enciende.**
The pilot light keeps going out.	**La luz piloto se apaga.**
Is there any danger of an explosion?	**¿Hay peligro de una explosión?**
I think the ventilator is blocked.	**Creo que el ventilador está obstruido.**
We can't get any hot water.	**No podemos obtener agua caliente.**

VOCABULARY

chimney	**la chimenea**
gas fire	**la estufa de gas**
gas light	**la luz de gas**
gas main	**la cañería maestra de gas**
gas pipe	**el tubo del gas**
gas tap	**la llave del gas**
geyser	**el calentador de agua**
hammer	**el martillo**
key	**la llave**
lagging	**el forro**
monkey wrench	**la llave inglesa**
spanner	**la llave de tuercas**
water heater	**el calentador de agua**

Plumbing

Are you the plumber?	**¿Es usted el fontanero?**
The sink/drain is stopped up.	**El fregadero/desagüe está cegado.**

There is a blockage in the pipe.	La cañería está bloqueada.
The tap is dripping.	La canilla gotea.
The tap needs a new washer.	La canilla necesita una arandela nueva.
This water pipe is leaking.	La cañería está goteando.
The lavatory cistern won't fill.	La cisterna del wáter no se llena.
The valve is stuck.	La válvula no se mueve.
The float is punctured.	El flotador está pinchado.
The water tank has run dry.	El tanque del agua está seco.
The tank is overflowing.	El tanque está rebosando.

Vocabulary

basin	el lavabo
bath	el baño
cesspool	el pozo negro
immersion heater	el calentador de inmersión
mains drainage	el alcantarillado
mains water	la cañería principal
overflow pipe	la cañería de desagüe
plug	el tapón
stopcock	la llave de cierre

Personal Services

This section suggests useful phrases for such occasions as a visit to a doctor, dentist, hairdresser, hospital or beautician.

At the Doctor's

Can you recommend a doctor?	¿Me puede recomendar un médico?
Is there an English-speaking doctor in the resort?	¿Hay un médico que hable inglés en el lugar?
Where is the surgery?	¿Dónde está el consultorio?
I have an appointment. My name is ...	Tengo cita. Mi nombre es ...
Can the doctor come to the hotel/house?	¿Puede el médico venir al hotel/a la casa?
I'm not feeling well.	No me encuentro muy bien.
I feel sick/dizzy/faint/shivery.	Me encuentro enfermo/mareado/débil/con escalofríos.
The pain is here.	Tengo el dolor aquí.

I have a temperature.
    headache.
    back ache.
    sore throat.
    sunburn.
	Tengo fiebre.
	    dolor de cabeza.
	    dolor de espalda.
	    dolor de garganta.
	    quemadura de sol.

I have been like this since yesterday.	Estoy así desde ayer.
I have been vomiting.	He estado devolviendo.
I have diarrhoea.	Tengo diarrea.

I am constipated.	**Estoy estreñido.**
I have hurt my ...	**Me he hecho daño en mi ...**
Do you want me to remove my clothes?	**¿Quiere que me quite la ropa?**
Is it serious?	**¿Es grave?**
Should I stay in bed?	**¿Debo de guardar cama?**
Should I arrange to go home?	**¿Debo de irme a mi país?**
I am allergic to ...	**Tengo alergia a ...**
I have a heart condition.	**Sufro del corazón.**
I am asthmatic/diabetic.	**Tengo asma/diabetes.**
Do I have to pay for hospitalisation and medicines?	**¿Tengo que pagar por hospitalización y medicinas?**
It's only a slight problem.	**Es sólo un ligero problema.**

VOCABULARY

PARTS OF THE BODY

ankle	**el tobillo**
appendix	**el apéndice**
arm	**el brazo**
artery	**la arteria**
back	**la espalda**
bladder	**la vejiga**
blood	**la sangre**
bone	**el hueso**
bowels	**los intestinos**
breast	**el seno**
cheek	**la mejilla**
chest	**el pecho**
chin	**la barbilla**

collar bone	**la clavícula**
ear	**el oído**
elbow	**el codo**
eye	**el ojo**
face	**la cara**
finger	**el dedo**
foot	**el pie**
forehead	**la frente**
gland	**la glándula**
hand	**la mano**
heart	**el corazón**
heel	**el talón**
hip	**la cadera**
intestine	**el intestino**
jaw	**la mandíbula**
joint	**la articulación**
kidney	**el riñón**
knee	**la rodilla**
leg	**la pierna**
lip	**el labio**
liver	**el hígado**
lung	**el pulmón**
mouth	**la boca**
muscle	**el músculo**
neck	**el cuello**
nerve	**el nervio**
nose	**la nariz**
penis	**el pene**
rib	**la costilla**
shoulder	**el hombro**
skin	**la piel**
spine	**la espina**
stomach	**el estómago**
tendon	**el tendón**
thigh	**el muslo**
throat	**la garganta**
thumb	**el dedo gordo (de la mano)**

toe	el dedo (del pie)
tongue	la lengua
tonsils	las amígdalas
urine	la orina
vein	la vena
vagina	la vagina
womb	la matriz
wrist	la muñeca

INDISPOSITIONS

abscess	el absceso
asthma	el asma
bite (dog/insect)	la mordedura/picadura
blisters	las ampollas
boil	el furúnculo
burn/scald	la quemadura
chill	el resfriado
cold	el frío
convulsions	las convulsiones
cramp	el calambre
cut	la cortada
diabetes	la diabetes
diarrhoea	la diarrea
dizziness	el mareo
haemorrhoids	las hemorroides
hay fever	la fiebre del heno
indigestion	la indigestión
infection	la infección
inflammation	la inflamación
influenza	la gripe
irritation	la irritación
nausea	la náusea
piles	las almorranas
rash	la erupción
rheumatism	el reumatismo
scald	la escaldadura
shivers	el escalofrío

Personal Services

stiff neck	**la tortícolis**
sunstroke	**la insolación**
tonsillitis	**la amigdalitis**
ulcer	**la úlcera**
whooping cough	**la tosferina**
wound	**la herida**

At the Dentist's

I need an appointment as soon as possible.	**Necesito una cita tan pronto como sea posible.**
I have a toothache/an abscess.	**Tengo dolor de muelas/un flemón.**
Can you suggest a painkiller until I can see you?	**¿Puede sugerir algo para el dolor hasta que le vea a Usted?**
The bad tooth is at the front/back/side.	**El diente que me hace daño es el colmillo/la muela de atrás/la muela de un lado.**
Can you extract it?	**¿Lo puede sacar?**
Does it need a filling?	**¿Necesita un empaste?**
Can you put in a temporary filling?	**¿Puede poner un empaste temporalmente?**
Can I bite normally?	**¿Puedo morder como siempre?**
I'd prefer gas to an injection.	**Prefiero gas a una injección.**
My gums are bleeding.	**Me sangran las encías.**
I have broken my dentures.	**He roto mis dentaduras.**
What is your fee?	**¿Cuánto son sus honorarios?**

At the Optician's

I have broken my glasses.	**He roto mis gafas.**
Can you repair them temporarily?	**¿Las puede arreglar temporalmente?**
The lens is broken. Can you get a new one quickly?	**He roto la lente. ¿Puede reemplazarla pronto?**
Have you got contact lenses?	**¿Tiene lentes de contacto?**
I'd like a pair of tinted spectacles.	**Quisiera un par de gafas ahumadas.**
Do you sell binoculars/a magnifying glass/sunglasses?	**¿Tiene binoculares/una lupa/gafas de sol?**
I had better have an eye test.	**Será mejor que me gradúe la vista.**
I am shortsighted/longsighted.	**Soy corto de vista/présbita.**
How long will it take to make me some new glasses?	**¿Cuánto llevará hacerme unas gafas nuevas?**
How much will they cost?	**¿Cuánto van a costar?**

At the Chiropodist's

I have a painful corn.	**Me duele un callo.**
Can you remove it?	**¿Me lo puede quitar?**
My bunion is rubbing against my shoe.	**El zapato me roza el juanete.**
I have a hard spot on the ball of my foot.	**Tengo un punto duro en la bola del pie.**
My nails need attention. One of them is ingrowing.	**Necesito que me atienda las uñas. Tengo un uñero.**

Personal Services

Have you anything to soften them?	¿Tiene algo para ablandarlas?
The soles of my feet are very sore.	Las plantas de mis pies están muy doloridas.

At the Hairdresser's

Where is the nearest hairdresser? Is there one in the hotel?	¿Dónde está el peluquero más cercano? ¿Hay uno en el hotel?
I'd like to make an appointment.	¿Me puede dar hora?
I want it cut and shaped.	Lo quiero cortado y con forma.
shampooed and set.	lavado y marcado.
I wear it brushed forward with a fringe.	Lo llevo peinado hacia delante y con un flequillo.
I like it brushed back.	Me gusta peinado hacia atrás.
Can you put some waves/curls in?	¿Me puede marcar ondas/hacer rizos?
Draw it back into a bun.	Recójalo atrás en un moño.
I'd like the ends bleached.	Me gustaría las puntas aclaradas.
Can you give me a colour rinse?	¿Me puede dar reflejos?
I think I will have it dyed.	Creo que me lo teñiré.
Have you got a colour chart?	¿Tiene un cuadro de colores?
No hairspray, thank you.	Nada de laca, gracias.
I'd like a manicure.	Quisiera una manicura.
What is the name of this nail varnish?	¿Cómo se llama este esmalte?

VOCABULARY

auburn	**castaño**
blond	**rubio**
brunette	**moreno**
brush	**el cepillo**
comb	**el peine**
to comb	**peinar**
drier	**el secador**
ginger	**pelirrojo**
hairnet	**la redecilla**
hairpiece	**el pelo postizo**
hair pin	**la horquilla**
razor	**la navaja**
rollers	**los rollos**
scissors	**las tijeras**
shampoo	**el champú**
styling	**el estilo**
wig	**la peluca**

At the Beauty Salon

I'd like a complete beauty treatment, please.

Quisiera un tratamiento de belleza, por favor.

just a facial.

solo un masaje facial.

to change my make-up.

cambiar mi maquillaje.

something more suitable for the seaside.

algo más conveniente para la playa.

something lighter in tone.

algo mas ligero de tono.

a more open-air look.

un aspecto más ligero.

Can you please suggest a new eye make-up?

¿Me puede sugerir un maquillaje nuevo para los ojos?

I have a delicate skin.

Tengo una piel delicada.

Personal Services

I think that is too heavy.	**Me parece demasiado pesado.**
Have you any false eyelashes?	**¿Tiene pestañas postizas?**
Perhaps my eyebrows need plucking.	**Quizás mis cejas necesitan depilación.**
I'd like to see some new lipstick colours.	**Quisiera ver colores nuevos de pintalabios.**

At the Laundry/Cleaner's

I'd like them washed/cleaned and pressed, please.	**Los quiero lavados/limpios y planchados, por favor.**
Will this stain come out? It is coffee/blood/grease/biro.	**¿Se quitará esta mancha? Es café/sangre/grasa/bolígrafo.**
Will you iron the shirts?	**¿Puede planchar las camisas?**
I will collect them tomorrow.	**Las recogeré mañana.**
Do you deliver?	**¿Hacen entrega?**
Do you do mending?	**¿Hacen remiendos?**
This tear needs patching.	**Este rasgón necesita un remiendo.**
Can you sew this button on?	**¿Puede coser este botón?**
Can you mend this invisibly?	**¿Puede hacer en esto un remiendo invisible?**
This blouse/coat/dress is not mine.	**Esta blusa/abrigo/vestido no es mía/mío.**
My trousers are missing.	**Faltan mis pantalones.**
This was not torn when I brought it to you.	**Esto no estaba rasgado cuando se lo traje.**

How long does the launderette stay open?	**¿Hasta cuando está abierta la lavandería automática?**

Vocabulary

bleach	**la lejía**
cleaning fluid	**el quitamanchas**
clothes hanger	**la percha**
cold/hot/warm water	**el agua fría/caliente/templada**
launderette	**la lavandería automática**
to press	**planchar**
rinse	**aclarar**
soap powder	**el jabón en polvo**
spin dry	**secar con centrífuga**
tumble dry	**secar completamente**
(the) washing	**el lavado**
washing machine	**la máquina de lavar**

At the Men's Hairdresser's

I want a haircut, please.	**Quiero un corte de pelo, por favor.**
Just a trim. I haven't much time.	**Sólo recortar las puntas. No tengo mucho tiempo.**
Please give me a shampoo.	**Un lavado de cabeza, por favor.**
I would like it cut shorter.	**Me gustaría más corto.**
Leave it long.	**Dejelo largo.**
You are taking too much off.	**Me está cortando mucho.**
Take a little more off the back/sides/top.	**Quite un poco más por atrás/por los lados/por arriba.**

Personal Services

I part my hair on the left/right.	**Me hago la raya en la izquierda/derecha.**
I'd like an alcohol rub/a singe.	**Quisiera una fricción de alcohol/un quemado de puntas.**
Please give me a shave.	**Me afeite, por favor.**
Please trim my beard/moustache/sideboards.	**Recorte mi barba/mi bigote/mis patillas, por favor.**
No thank you, I do not want a facial massage.	**No gracias, no quiero un masaje facial.**
I will have a manicure.	**Me haga la manicura.**
May I have a hand towel?	**¿Me puede dar una toalla de las manos?**
Put some eau de cologne on but no cream.	**Deme agua de colonia, pero no crema.**
Move the mirror a bit more to the right.	**Mueva el espejo un poco más a la derecha.**
Yes, that's fine.	**Si, así está bien.**

Making Friends

Good morning/good afternoon/good evening.	Buenos días/buenas tardes/buenas tardes/noches.
May I introduce myself? my friend John? my wife?	Permítame que me presente. le presente a mi amigo John. le presente a mi esposa.
I am ...	Me llamo ...
How do you do?	Tanto gusto en conocerle.
Are you staying at this hotel/at this resort?	¿Reside en este hotel/este lugar?
Are you enjoying your holiday?	¿Está pasando bien las vacaciones?
How long have you been on holiday?	¿Cuánto tiempo hace que está de vacaciones?
Do you always come here?	¿Viene siempre aquí?
I'd like you to meet my friend.	Quisiera presentarle a mi amigo.
Would you care to have a drink with us?	¿Quiere tomar algo con nosotros?
What would you like?	¿Qúe quiere?
Please. I insist that you let me pay.	Por favor. Insisto en que me deje pagar.
I'm afraid that I don't speak Spanish very well.	Lo siento pero no hablo muy bien el español.
It is very nice to talk to a Spanish person.	Es muy agradable hablar con una persona española.

Making Friends

Which part of Spain do you come from? | ¿De qué parte de España es?

I am here with my wife/husband/family/friends. | Estoy aquí con mi esposa/marido/familia/mis amigos.

Are you alone? | ¿Está usted solo (sola)?

We come from Manchester/England. | Somos de Manchester/Inglaterra.

Have you been to England? | ¿Ha estado en Inglaterra?

If you come, please le me know. | Me diga si viene.

This is my address. | Esta es mi dirección.

I hope to see you again soon. | Espero verle pronto.

Perhaps you would like to meet for a drink after dinner? | Quizás nos podamos encontrar para tomar algo después de la cena.

I would be delighted to join you. | Con mucho gusto.

At what time shall I come? | ¿A qué hora vengo?

Have you got a family? | ¿Tiene familia?

Would you like to see some photos of our house/our children? | ¿Quiere ver una fotos de nuestra casa/nuestros hijos?

Are you going to the gala? | ¿Va a la fiesta?

Would you like to make up a party? | ¿Le gustaría unirse a un grupo?

It has been very nice to meet you. | Estoy encantado de conocerle.

You have been very kind. | Es usted muy amable.

Dating Someone

Are you on holiday?	¿Está de vacaciones?
Do you live here?	¿Vive aquí?
Do you like this place?	¿Le gusta este sitio?
I've just arrived.	Acabo de llegar.
What is there to do?	¿Qué se puede hacer?
I don't know anyone here.	No conozco aquí a nadie.
I'm with a lot of students.	Estoy con un grupo de estudiantes.
I'm travelling alone.	Estoy viajando solo (sola).
I'm on my way round Europe.	Estoy viajando por Europa.
I come from Scotland/Australia/New Zealand/the United States.	Soy de Escocia/Australia/Nueva Zelanda/los Estados Unidos.
Do you mind if I try my Spanish on you?	¿Le importa si practico mi español con usted?
My Spanish is not very good.	Mi español no es muy bueno.
Would you like a drink?	¿Quiere tomar algo?
What are you doing this evening?	¿Qúe hace esta noche?
Would you like to go to a discotheque?	¿Le gustaría ir a una discoteca?
join our party?	unirse a nuestro grupo?
Do you like dancing/concerts/opera?	¿Le gusta bailar/los conciertos/la ópera?
Can I walk along with you?	¿Puedo acompañarle?
Which way are you going?	¿Por dónde va?

Making Friends

Do you mind if I sit here?	¿Le importa que me siente aquí?
This is my friend, Tom.	Este es mi amigo, Tom.
Do you have a girl friend?	¿Tiene novia?
We could make a foursome.	Podíamos hacer un grupo de cuatro.
Do you play tennis/golf?	¿Juega al tenis/golf?
Do you go swimming?	¿Va a nadar?
Which beach do you go to?	¿A qué playa va?
Would you like to come for a drive/boat ride?	¿Le gustaría dar una vuelta en coche/en lancha?
It would be nice if you would.	Será estupendo si viene.
Thanks for coming out with me.	Gracias por salir conmigo.
I enjoyed it.	Lo he pasado bien.
Can we meet again?	¿Le puedo ver de nuevo?
How about tomorrow?	¿Mañana?
No thanks, I'm busy.	No, gracias, estoy ocupado(a).
Please stop bothering me.	Deje de molestarme.

Mutual Interest

Do you play cards?	¿Juega a las cartas?
Would you like to make a four at bridge?	¿Le gustaría hacer de cuatro al bridge?
We play canasta/poker/rummy.	Jugamos a la canasta/al póker/al rummy.
It is an English game.	Es un juego inglés.

Are you a chess player?	¿Es jugador de ajedrez?
I'll ask the concierge if the hotel has a chess-board.	Le preguntaré al conserje si hay un tablero de ajedrez en el hotel.
This is your king/queen/knight/bishop/castle/pawn.	Este es su rey/reina/caballo/alfil/torre/peón.
We could play draughts or dominoes.	Podíamos jugar a las damas o al dominó.
There is a table tennis table in the hotel. Would you care for a game?	Hay una mesa de tenis en el hotel. ¿Le gustaría jugar una partida?
Do you read English?	¿Puede leer inglés?
Would you like to borrow this book/newspaper?	¿Le puedo prestar este libro/periódico?

Spanish playing cards are different from the conventional deck, although these are also used. The Spanish deck consists of four suits: **copa**, shown as a drinking goblet; **bastones**, a wooden club; **espadas**, swords, and **oros**, gold pieces. The suits are numbered from one to seven and the court cards are page, knight (instead of queen) and king (**sota/caballo/rey**)

Conversations

There are certain universal subjects of conversation which provide a bridge for communication with strangers all over the world. Among these are the weather, families, home, the cost of living, and pets. The following conversational phrases are designed to start you off on an acquaintanceship with people who do not speak English.

About the Weather

It is a fine day.	**Hace un día bueno.**
It's not a very nice day.	**No es un día muy bueno.**
Will it rain all day/later/ tomorrow, do you think?	**¿Cree que lloverá todo el día/ más tarde/mañana?**
It's going to be hot/cold today.	**Va a hacer calor/frío hoy.**
It's rather windy.	**Hace bastante viento.**
I think there is a thunderstorm coming.	**Creo que se aproxima una tormenta.**
Look at the lightning.	**Mire los relámpagos.**
It will soon clear up.	**Se pasará pronto.**
We don't get this kind of weather at home.	**No tenemos esta clase de tiempo en mi país.**
It's a pity it is so dull.	**Es una pena que esté tan gris.**
Did you see the beautiful sunrise/sunset?	**¿Vió la salida de sol/puesta de sol tan bonita?**
We had a very good/very poor summer last year.	**Tuvimos un verano muy bueno/muy malo el año pasado.**
There's a lot of haze about today.	**Hay mucha neblina hoy.**
The atmosphere is very clear.	**La atmósfera está muy despejada.**
It is cold here in the winter?	**¿Hace frío aquí en el invierno?**
I love the spring/summer/ autumn.	**Me gusta la primavera/el verano/el otoño.**
What does the barometer say?	**¿Qué marca el barómetro?**

VOCABULARY

breeze	**la brisa**
cloudburst	**el chaparrón**
cloudy	**nublado**
drizzle	**la llovizna**
dry	**seco**
forecast	**el pronóstico**
hail	**el granizo**
meteorological office	**la oficina meteorológica**
mist	**la niebla**
office	**la oficina**
pressure	**la presión**
raining	**lloviendo**
sleet	**el aguanieve**
snow	**la nieve**
sunny	**soleado**
temperature	**la temperatura**
weather report	**el boletín meteorológico**
wet	**húmedo**

About Families

This is my wife/husband/ daughter/son.	**Esta(e) es mi esposa/marido/ hija/hijo.**
My son is an architect/doctor/ student/teacher/engineer.	**Mi hijo es arquitecto/médico/ estudiante/maestro/ ingeniero.**
My daughter is at school.	**Mi hija va al colegio.**
She is taking her examinations. Then she will go to university/ art school/teacher's training college.	**Está de exámenes. Después irá a la universidad/ a la escuela de arte/al magisterio.**

Making Friends

She learnt some Spanish at school.	**Aprendió algo de español en el colegio.**
My wife is Scottish, but her mother is Spanish.	**Mi esposa es escocesa, pero su madre es española.**
My father was a teacher.	**Mi padre fue profesor.**
The children prefer to have holidays on their own.	**Los hijos prefieren ir de vacaciones solos.**
They prefer camping.	**Prefieren ir de camping.**
My eldest/youngest son/ daughter is married and lives in ...	**Mi hijo/hija mayor/menor está casado(a) y vive en ...**
Would you like to see some photos of our family?	**¿Quiere ver unas fotos de nuestra familia?**
The younger children stayed at home with their grandparents.	**Los hijos más pequeños se quedaron en casa con los abuelos.**
Are these your children?	**¿Son estos sus hijos?**
The boy/girl looks like his/her mother/father.	**El niño/niña se parece a su madre/padre.**
How old is he/she?	**¿Cuántos años tiene?**
My daughter is fourteen.	**Mi hija tiene catorce años.**

VOCABULARY

aunt	**la tía**
birthday	**el cumpleaños**
cousin	**el primo/la prima**
divorce	**el divorcio**
in-law	**político**
marriage	**el matrimonio**

relatives	**los parientes**
uncle	**el tío**
wedding	**la boda**

About Homes

We have a house in town/in the country.	**Tenemos una casa en la ciudad/en el campo.**
It is a detached two-storey house.	**Es una casa independiente de dos pisos.**
semi-detached.	**semiseparada.**
a cottage.	**un chalet.**
a maisonette.	**una casita.**
a flat.	**un piso.**
We have a large garden/a patio.	**Tenemos un jardín grande/un patio.**
There are two living rooms. One has a French window and the other a bay window.	**Hay dos salas de estar. Una tiene una puerta ventana y la otra un mirador.**
There is a fireplace in the dining room.	**Hay una chimenea en el comedor.**
The whole house is centrally heated/air conditioned.	**Toda la casa tiene calefacción central/aire acondicionado.**
We have two garages.	**Tenemos dos garajes.**
The back garden has a lawn and swimming pool.	**El jardín de atrás tiene un césped y una piscina.**
In our village there are many old houses.	**En nuestro pueblo hay muchas casas viejas.**
We prefer a modern/old house.	**Preferimos una casa moderna/vieja.**

Making Friends

What kind of house have you got?	¿Qué clase de casa tiene?
I like Spanish-style houses.	Me gustan las casas de estilo español.
Do you cook by gas or electricity?	¿Cocinan con gas o electricidad?
In a warm climate tiled floors are delightful.	Los pisos de baldosas son estupendos en un clima templado.
Wall to wall carpeting makes a house warm in winter.	Alfombras de lado a lado de la pared hacen la casa caliente en el invierno.
Built-in cupboards make a room seem larger.	Los armarios empotrados hacen parecer una habitación más grande.
Old furniture is lovely but very expensive.	Los muebles antiguos son muy bonitos pero muy caros.

VOCABULARY

balcony	el balcón
brick	el ladrillo
ceiling	el techo
chimney	la chimenea
door	la puerta
drains	los desagües
foundations	los cimientos
gable	el gablete
mains electricity/water	la red eléctrica/cañería principal
plumbing	las cañerías
roof	el tejado
stone	la piedra

terrace	**la terraza**
thatch	**la paja**
tiles	**las baldosas**
wall	**la pared**
window	**la ventana**
window frame	**el marco de la ventana**
window pane	**el cristal**
wood	**la madera**

On Business

I have an appointment with the Manager.	**Tengo una cita con el director.**
I am from Smith and Company.	**Soy de Smith y Compañía.**
Here is my card.	**Aquí está mi tarjeta.**
It is good of you to see me.	**Es muy amable en recibirme.**
May I show you our catalogue/samples?	**¿Puedo enseñarle nuestro catálogo/nuestras muestras?**
My company manufactures knitwear.	**Mi compañía confecciona géneros de punto.**
We are looking for agents.	**Buscamos representantes.**
Our wholesale prices/retail prices are on this list.	**Nuestros precios de venta al por mayor/menor están en esta lista.**
There is a special discount for a large quantity.	**Hay un descuento especial por grandes cantidades.**
Delivery is within four weeks/six months/immediate.	**La entrega será dentro de cuatro semanas/seis meses/inmediata.**

On Business

The prices are f.o.b.	**Los precios son franco a bordo.**
I would like to see your products.	**Quisiera ver sus productos.**
Have you a showroom in the town?	**¿Tiene una sala de exposición en la ciudad?**
What are your terms of business?	**¿Cuál es su plazo de negocios?**
Do you already have agents in my country?	**¿Tiene ya representantes en mi país?**
Can you make modifications to this model?	**¿Puede hacer modificaciones en este modelo?**
May I take some samples with me?	**¿Puedo llevarme unas muestras?**
I will give you an order now.	**Le haré un pedido ahora.**
Can you look after the packing and shipping?	**¿Puede ocuparse del embalaje y transporte en barco?**
There is only a small market for these goods.	**Hay un mercado muy pequeño para estos géneros.**

VOCABULARY

balance sheet	**el balance**
banker	**el banquero**
bill	**la factura**
bill of exchange	**la letra de cambio**
certificate	**el certificado**
clerk	**el empleado**
contract	**el contrato**
correspondence	**la correspondencia**

credit	**el crédito**
debit	**el debe**
draft	**el giro/la letra de cambio**
export	**la exportación**
freight	**las mercancías**
import	**el importe**
insurance	**el seguro**
invoice	**la factura**
merchant	**el comerciante**
receipt	**el recibo**
remittance	**el envío**
sale	**la venta**
warehouse	**el almacén**

Looking After your Money

The Bank

Where is the nearest bank?	¿Dónde está el banco más cercano?
Do you accept travellers' cheques at this bank?	¿Aceptan cheques de viajero en este banco?
Can I use a Eurocheque card?	¿Puedo utilizar una tarjeta Eurocheque?
Do you issue money against a credit card?	¿Puede darme dinero en efectivo con una tarjeta de crédito?
I am expecting a remittance.	Espero una transferencia.
I have a letter of credit.	Tengo una garantía bancaria.
I would like a draft to send away.	Quisiera una letra de cambio para mandar fuera.
What is the rate of exchange for the pound/dollar/Australian dollar?	¿A cómo está el cambio de la libra/el dólar/el dólar australiano?
What is your commission charge?	¿Cuánto cargan de comisión?
I will have it all in 100 peseta notes.	Me lo de todo en billetes de cien pesetas.
Please give me 50 pesetas' worth of change.	Por favor, me de cincuenta pesetas en calderilla.
Can you split this cheque into several currencies?	¿Puede pagarme este cheque en diversas monedas extranjeras?

I will have some German marks, Swiss francs and Spanish pesetas.	Me de marcos alemanes, francos suizos y pesetas.
Can I open a temporary bank account?	¿Puedo abrir una cuenta temporalmente?
Can you arrange for some money to be sent from my bank in Britain?	¿Puede arreglar para que transfieran dinero de mi banco en Inglaterra?
I seem to be ten francs short. Can you please count it again?	Me parece que me ha dado diez francos de menos. ¿Lo puede contar de nuevo?
Have you a card showing current exchange rates?	¿Tiene una lista al corriente con los tipos de cambio?

VOCABULARY

Bank of England	el Banco de Inglaterra
cashier	el cajero
cheque book	el talonario de cheques
coins	las monedas
credit	el crédito
debit	el debe
deposit slip	la papeleta de depósito
foreign exchange regulations	las regulaciones de divisas
manager	el director
notes	los billetes
signature	la firma
treasury	la hacienda

Money Matters

COINS   10 céntimos
                  50 céntimos
                  1 peseta
                  5 pesetas
                  50 pesetas
                  100 pesetas

NOTES   100 pesetas
                  500 pesetas
                  1,000 pesetas

Bureau de Change

Are you open outside banking hours?	¿Está abierto fuera de las horas bancarias?
Does the rate of exchange alter outside normal hours?	¿Altera el índice de cambio fuera de las horas normales?
Are you open on Sundays?	¿Abren los domingos?
Can you show me your rates of exchange?	¿Me puede enseñar los índices de cambio?
Do you give the same rate for notes as for travellers' cheques?	¿Paga el mismo precio por billetes que por cheques de viajero?

On Losing Travellers' Cheques or Credit Cards

When this happens you should immediately notify the company that has issued the cheques or card but you may need help from a local hotelier or banker.

I have lost my travellers' cheques/credit card.	He perdido mis billetes de viajero/mi tarjeta de crédito.

May I ask them to communicate with me through you?

¿Puedo decirles que se comuniquen conmigo por medio de ustedes?

Have you a British representative?

¿Tienen un representante británico?

I hope they will be able to refund the cheques quickly. I have no other money.

Espero que me puedan re-embolsar los cheques rapidamente. No tengo otro dinero.

I will ask my bank at home to send some money to you.

Pediré a mi banco que les envíen dinero.

Will you accept a British cheque in payment of the hotel bill?

¿Pueden aceptar un cheque inglés como pago de la cuenta del hotel?

Reference Section

Numbers

1	uno
2	dos
3	tres
4	cuatro
5	cinco
6	seis
7	siete
8	ocho
9	nueve
10	diez
11	once
12	doce
13	trece
14	catorce
15	quince
16	dieciséis
17	diecisiete
18	dieciocho
19	diecinueve
20	veinte
21	veintiuno
22	veintidós
23	veintitrés
24	veinticuatro
25	veinticinco
26	veintiséis
27	veintisiete
28	veintiocho
29	veintinueve
30	treinta
31	treinta y uno
32	treinta y dos

33	treinta y tres
34	treinta y cuatro
35	treinta y cinco
36	treinta y seis
37	treinta y siete
40	cuarenta
50	cincuenta
60	sesenta
70	setenta
80	ochenta
90	noventa
100	cien
101	ciento uno
110	ciento diez
200	dos cientos
1000	mil
1001	mil uno
1100	mil cien
2000	dos mil
1,000,000	un millón
1,000,000,000	mil millones

first	primero
second	segundo
third	tercero
fourth	cuarto
fifth	quinto
sixth	sexto
seventh	séptimo
eighth	octavo
ninth	noveno
tenth	décimo

once	una vez
twice	dos veces
three times	tres veces

half	**medio**
quarter	**cuarto**
third	**tercio**
eighth	**octavo**
a pair of	**un par de**
a dozen	**una docena**
a gross	**una gruesa**

Phrases Referring to Numbers

Two heads are better than one.	**Dos cabezas piensan mejor que una.**
Two and two make four.	**Dos y dos son cuatro.**
The last shall be first.	**Los últimos serán los primeros.**

Time

Greenwich Mean time	**horario de Greenwich**
Central European time	**horario centroeuropeo**
Atlantic time	**horario atlántico**
Date line	**línea de cambio de fecha**
AM/PM	**antes/después del medio día**
24-hour clock	**reloj de veinticuatro horas**
summer time	**horario de verano**
it is 12.15	**son las doce y cuarto**
it is 12.20	**son las doce y veinte**
it is 12.30	**son las doce y media**
it is 12.35	**es la una menos veinticinco**
it is 12.45	**es la una menos cuarto**
it is 1.00	**es la una**
midnight	**medianoche**
midday	**mediodía**

Phrases Referring to Time

What time is it?	**¿Qué hora es?**
It is late.	**Es tarde.**
It is early.	**Es pronto.**
Are we on time?	**¿Estamos a tiempo?**
At what time shall we meet?	**¿A qué hora nos encontramos?**
At what time are we expected?	**¿A qué hora nos esperan?**
On the hour.	**A la hora en punto.**
Day by day.	**Día tras día.**
By the minute.	**Por minuto.**
Every second.	**Cada segundo.**

At regular intervals.	**A intervalos regulares.**
After the clock strikes.	**Después que el reloj de la hora.**
Days, weeks and years.	**Días, semanas y años.**
Sunday	**domingo**
Monday	**lunes**
Tuesday	**martes**
Wednesday	**miércoles**
Thursday	**jueves**
Friday	**viernes**
Saturday	**sábado**
daybreak	**amanecer**
dawn	**amanecer**
morning	**mañana**
afternoon	**tarde**
evening	**tarde**
night	**noche**
today	**hoy**
yesterday	**ayer**
tomorrow	**mañana**
the day before yesterday	**antes de ayer**
two days ago	**hace dos días**
the day after tomorrow	**pasado mañana**
the following day	**el día siguiente**
weekday	**día laborable**
a day off	**día libre**
birthday	**cumpleaños**
Christmas Day	**Navidad**
New Year's Day	**Año Nuevo**
All Saints' Day	**Todos los Santos**
May Day	**primero de mayo**
weekend	**fin de semana**
last week	**la semana pasada**
next week	**la semana próxima**
for two weeks	**por dos semanas**

January	**enero**
February	**febrero**
March	**marzo**
April	**abril**
May	**mayo**
June	**junio**
July	**julio**
August	**agosto**
September	**septiembre**
October	**octubre**
November	**noviembre**
December	**diciembre**
calendar month	**mes**
lunar month	**mes lunar**
monthly	**mensualmente**
since January	**desde enero**
last month	**el mes pasado**
next month	**el mes próximo**
the month before	**el mes anterior**
the first of the month	**el primero de mes**
the first of March	**el uno de marzo**
spring	**primavera**
summer	**verano**
autumn	**otoño**
winter	**invierno**
years	**años**
BC	**antes de Jesucristo**
AD	**después de Jesucristo**
leap year	**año bisiesto**

Temperature Equivalents

FAHRENHEIT		CENTIGRADE
212	Boiling point	100
100		37·8
98·4	Body temperature	37
86		30
77		25
68		20
50		10
32	Freezing point	0
0		−18

To convert Fahrenheit to Centigrade subtract 32 and divide by 1·8. To convert Centigrade to Fahrenheit multiply by 1·8 and add 32.

Pressure

The barometer tells you the air pressure of the atmosphere. 15 lb. per sq. in. is normal air pressure at sea level. This equals 1·1 kg. per sq. cm.

A tyre gauge tells you the pressure of your car tyres.

POUNDS PER SQUARE INCH	KILOGRAMS PER SQUARE CENTIMETRE
16	1·12
18	1·17
20	1·41
22	1·55
24	1·69
26	1·83
28	1·97

Measurements of Distance

One kilometre = 1000 metres = 0·62 miles

One hundred centimetres = 1 metre = 3·3 feet

One centimetre = 0·39 inches.

The following tables gives equivalents for metres and feet. The figure in the centre column can stand for either feet or metres and the equivalent should then be read off in the appropriate column.

METRES	METRES AND FEET	FEET
0·30	1	3·28
0·61	2	6·56
0·91	3	9·84
1·12	4	13·12
1·52	5	16·40
1·83	6	19·68
2·13	7	22·97
2·44	8	26·25
2·74	9	29·53
3·05	10	32·81
3·35	11	36·09
3·66	12	39·37
3·96	13	42·65
4·27	14	45·93
4·57	15	49·21
4·88	16	52·49
5·18	17	55·77
5·49	18	59·05
5·79	19	62·34
6·10	20	65·62
7·62	25	82·02
15·24	50	164·04
22·86	75	246·06
30·48	100	328·08

MILES	MILES AND KILOMETRES	KILOMETRES
0.62	1	1·61
1·24	2	3·22
1·86	3	4·82
2·49	4	6·44
3·11	5	8·05
3·73	6	9·66
4·35	7	11·27
4·97	8	12·88
5·59	9	14·48
6·21	10	16·09
15·53	25	40·23
31·07	50	80.47
46·60	75	120·70
62·14	100	160·93

For motorists it is useful to remember that:

30 miles = 48·3 km.

70 miles = 112·7 km.

70 km. = 43·75 miles

100 km. = 62·50 miles

To convert kilometres to miles, divide by 8 and multiply by 5.

To convert miles to kilometres, divide by 5 and multiply by 8.

Measurements of Quantity
Weight

POUNDS	POUNDS AND KILOGRAMS	KILOGRAMS
2·20	1	0·45
4·40	2	0·90
6·61	3	1·36
8·82	4	1·81
11·02	5	2·27
13·23	6	2·72
15·43	7	3·18
17·64	8	3·63

OUNCES	GRAMS
0·5	14·12
1	28·35
2	56·70
3	85·05
4	113·40
5	141·75
6	170·10
7	198·45
8 (½ lb.)	226·80
12	340·19
16 (1 lb.)	453·59

One kilogram = 1000 grams = 2·2 lb.

Half a kilogram = 500 grams = 1·1 lb.

When shopping for small items, Spanish people usually order by the 100 grams; this is about 3½ ounces.

One metric ton = 1000 kilograms.

Liquid Measures

UK PINTS	UK PINTS AND LITRES	LITRES
1·76	1	0·57
3·52	2 (1 quart)	1·14
5·28	3	1·70
7·04	4	2·27
8·80	5	2·84
10·56	6	3·41
12·32	7	3·98
14·08	8 (1 gallon)	4·55
15·84	9	5·11
17·60	10	5·68

1 litre = 1·76 pints.

One tenth of a litre = 1 decilitre or ·18 of a pint.

One hundredth of a litre = 1 centilitre or ·018 of a pint.

One hundred litres = 1 hectolitre or 22 gallons.

One gallon = 4·6 litres.

One quart = 1·136 litres.

One pint = 0·57 litre.

Clothing Sizes

Measurements for clothes are measured according to the metric system. Here are the sizes for the main articles of clothing.

Women

DRESSES AND SUITS

British	34	36	38	40	42	44	46
American	32	34	36	38	40	42	44
Continental	40	42	44	46	48	50	52

Men

SUITS

British and American	36	38	40	42	44	46
Continental	46	48	50	52	54	56

SHIRTS

British and American	14	14½	15	15½	16	16½	17
Continental	36	37	38	39	41	42	43

Index

Index

S
S...,
Spanish

2

Essential
Spanish Words

Des Meagher
Beverley Roberts

Super Simple Spanish ™

This edition first published in 2014.

ISBN 13 978-0-9552198-8-7

Printed and bound in Spain.

For more information about the
Super Simple Spanish series of books
please see our website:

www.supersimplespanish.com

Contents

Introduction

The Super Simple Spanish series of books is designed to make Spanish as simple as possible.

Super Simple Spanish No 2 Essential Words has:

Spanish Vocabulary
Over 1200 basic and essential Spanish words grouped together under 75 useful headings.

Spanish Pronunciation
Simple Spanish pronunciation and how word stress is used.

Spain Guide
The highlights of Spain with maps of mainland Spain and the Spanish Islands.

The Authors

We love Spain. We try and visit as often as we can. We've worked in Madrid and Seville and spent a small fortune on books over the years trying to improve our Spanish.

Some Spanish books are good and some are not so good. What all our Spanish books have in common is that they are in a drawer somewhere and we never use them. How does that happen?

We took another look at our Spanish books and the answer became clear. Very few of our Spanish books are simple and none of them are super simple. So, starting with vocabulary, we decided to produce a series of books that really would make Spanish Super Simple.

Super Simple Spanish

Each book in the Super Simple Spanish series gives you simple **Spanish Vocabulary**, simple **Spanish Pronunciation** and our **Spain Guide** highlighting the very best of Spain.

The first 3 books in this series are:

No 1. Similar Words
Over 1200 useful words that are amazingly similar in Spanish and English.

No 2. Essential Words
Over 1200 basic and essential Spanish words grouped together under 75 simple headings.

No 3. Important Words
Over 1200 important Spanish words carefully chosen to expand your Spanish vocabulary.

SPANISH VOCABULARY

Basic
Spanish Words
(1-13)

Essential
Spanish Words
(14-106)

PLEASE NOTE

The Spanish Words section has many Spanish words that end in o. Words ending in o are usually masculine in Spanish.

There are also many words that end in a in Spanish and these words are usually feminine.

Some Spanish words can end in o or a if they are used in the masculine and the feminine.

For example,

    amigo = male friend
    amiga = female friend

    camarero = waiter
    camarera = waitress

To keep the Spanish Vocabulary section as simple as possible we have used the masculine ending o for words that can be used in the masculine and the feminine.

BASICS 1

yes	sí
no	no
please	por favor
thank you	gracias
okay	vale
excuse me	perdón
sorry	lo siento
you're welcome	de nada

BASICS 2

hello	hola
good morning	buenos días
good afternoon	buenas tardes
good evening	buenas tardes
goodnight	buenas noches
goodbye	adiós
see you later	hasta luego
see you tomorrow	hasta mañana

BASICS 3

airport	aeropuerto
taxi	taxi
bus	autobús
train	tren
underground	metro
ticket	billete
bus station	estación de autobuses
train station	estación de trenes

BASICS 4

tourist office	oficina de turismo
information	información
town map	plano
timetable	horario
hotel	hotel
restaurant	restaurante
toilets	servicios
Ladies	Señoras
Gents	Caballeros

BASICS 5

town	ciudad
town centre	centro ciudad
town hall	ayuntamiento
main square	plaza mayor
street	calle
church	iglesia
park	parque
river	río
bridge	puente
beach	playa

BASICS 6

shop	tienda
market	mercado
supermarket	supermercado
car park	parking
chemist's	farmacia
post office	Correos
shopping centre	centro comercial
department store	grandes almacenes

BASICS 7

accident	accidente
police	policía
ambulance	ambulancia
fire brigade	bomberos
Red Cross	Cruz Roja
doctor	médico
dentist	dentista
hospital	hospital
accident & emergency	urgencias

BASICS 8

tea	té
coffee	café
milk	leche
sugar	azúcar
hot chocolate	chocolate
saccharin	sacarina
beer	cerveza
wine	vino
juice	zumo
water	agua

BASICS 9

bread	pan
butter	mantequilla
toast	tostada
jam	mermelada
honey	miel
eggs	huevos
bacon	bacon
sausage	salchicha
ham	jamón
cheese	queso

BASICS 10

big	grande
small	pequeño
hot	caliente
cold	frío
a lot	mucho
a little	poco
more	más
less	menos
with	con
without	sin

BASICS 11

today	hoy
tomorrow	mañana
yesterday	ayer
now	ahora
soon	pronto
later	más tarde
before	antes
after	después
here	aquí
there	allí

BASICS 12

Monday	lunes
Tuesday	martes
Wednesday	miércoles
Thursday	jueves
Friday	viernes
Saturday	sábado
Sunday	domingo
day	día
week	semana
weekend	fin de semana

BASICS 13

Where is..?	¿Dónde está..?
How much..?	¿Cuánto..?
What time..?	¿A qué hora..?
Is there...?	¿Hay..?
Are there...?	¿Hay..?
What's your name?	¿Cómo se llama?
Where are you from?	¿De dónde es?
Do you speak English?	¿Habla inglés?

AIRPORT

airport	aeropuerto
arrivals	llegadas
departures	salidas
passport	pasaporte
ticket	billete
suitcase	maleta
luggage	equipaje
information	información
flight	vuelo
gate	puerta
foreign exchange	cambio

ANIMALS

animal	animal
bird	ave
dog	perro
cat	gato
horse	caballo
cow	vaca
sheep	oveja
pig	cerdo
chicken	pollo
rabbit	conejo
bull	toro
goat	cabra

APARTMENT

apartment	apartamento
building	edificio
flat	piso
penthouse	ático
floor	planta
lift	ascensor
stairs	escalera
balcony	balcón
roof terrace	azotea
swimming pool	piscina
letter-box	buzón
rubbish	basura

BABY

baby	bebé
milk	leche
bottle	biberón
nappy	pañal
wet wipes	toallitas húmedas
changing mat	cambiador
pushchair	cochecito
high chair	trona
cot	cuna
babysitter	canguro
child seat	asiento de niño

BAGS

bag	bolsa
handbag	bolso
purse	monedero
wallet	cartera
backpack	mochila
holdall	bolsa de viaje
beach bag	bolsa de playa
briefcase	maletín
suitcase	maleta
luggage	equipaje
hand luggage	equipaje de mano

BANK

bank	banco
client	cliente
money	dinero
cash machine	cajero automático
cheque	cheque
transfer	transferencia
debit card	tarjeta de débito
credit card	tarjeta de crédito
commission	comisión
foreign exchange	cambio

BANK

current account	cuenta corriente
savings account	cuenta de ahorros
interest	interés
balance	saldo
payment	pago
mortgage	hipoteca
loan	préstamo
overdraft	descubierto
to deposit	ingresar
to withdraw	retirar / sacar

BATHROOM

bathroom	cuarto de baño
bath	bañera
shower	ducha
toilet	aseo
bidet	bidé
sink	lavabo
tap	grifo
plug	tapón
mirror	espejo
shower curtain	cortina de ducha
towel	toalla

BEACH

beach	playa
sun	sol
sea	mar
sand	arena
wave	ola
seashell	concha
flag	bandera
lifeguard	socorrista
beach bar	chiringuito
sunlounger	hamaca
beach umbrella	sombrilla

BEDROOM

bedroom	dormitorio
bed	cama
mattress	colchón
sheet	sábana
pillow	almohada
pillowcase	funda
duvet	edredón
blanket	manta
wardrobe	armario
coat hanger	percha
lamp	lámpara
alarm clock	despertador

BICYCLE

bicycle	bicicleta
saddle	sillín
gears	marchas
brake	freno
chain	cadena
pedal	pedal
wheel	rueda
tyre	cubierta
puncture	pinchazo
pump	bomba
helmet	casco
lock	candado

BODY

body	cuerpo
skin	piel
head	cabeza
neck	cuello
shoulder	hombro
back	espalda
chest	pecho
stomach	estómago
arm	brazo
leg	pierna
hand	mano
foot	pie

BODY

elbow	codo
wrist	muñeca
knee	rodilla
ankle	tobillo
finger	dedo
toe	dedo del pie
face	cara
eye	ojo
ear	oreja
nose	nariz
mouth	boca
tooth	diente

CAMPING

campsite	camping
camper	campista
pitch	plaza
tent	tienda
caravan	caravana
camper van	autocaravana
trailer	remolque
showers	duchas
electricity	electricidad
drinking water	agua potable
no vacancies	completo

CELEBRATIONS

celebration	celebración
party	fiesta
present	regalo
birthday	cumpleaños
engagement	compromiso
wedding	boda
honeymoon	luna de miel
anniversary	aniversario
retirement	jubilación
happy birthday	feliz cumpleaños
congratulations	enhorabuena

CHEMIST'S

chemist's	farmacia
cut	corte
bite	picadura
burn	quemadura
pain	dolor
allergy	alergia
nausea	náusea
aspirin	aspirina
paracetamol	paracetamol
antibiotic	antibiótico
antiseptic	antiséptico
plaster	tirita®

CLOTHES

clothes	ropa
coat	abrigo
jacket	chaqueta
shirt	camisa
trousers	pantalones
jumper	suéter
blouse	blusa
skirt	falda
dress	vestido
shoes	zapatos
shorts	pantalones cortos

CLOTHES

jeans	vaqueros
t-shirt	camiseta
belt	cinturón
tie	corbata
socks	calcetines
underwear	ropa interior
bra	sujetador
knickers	bragas
tights	medias
underpants	calzoncillos
swimwear	bañadores
pyjamas	pijama

COAST

coast	costa
beach	playa
sea	mar
shore	orilla
dune	duna
rock	roca
cove	cala
bay	bahía
island	isla
cape	cabo
lighthouse	faro
cliff	acantilado

COLOURS

colour	color
red	rojo
yellow	amarillo
blue	azul
green	verde
black	negro
white	blanco
grey	gris
pink	rosa
purple	morado
orange	naranja
brown	marrón

COMPUTERS

computer	ordenador
keyboard	teclado
mouse	ratón
monitor	monitor
screen	pantalla
hard drive	disco duro
software	software
program	programa
disk	disco
cable	cable
printer	impresora
ink	tinta

COOKING

cook	cocinero
meal	comida
homemade	casera
roast	asado
fried	frito
baked	al horno
grilled	a la parrilla
barbecued	a la brasa
on a hotplate	a la plancha
battered	a la romana
stuffed	relleno
smoked	ahumado

COUNTRIES

country	país
England	Inglaterra
Scotland	Escocia
Wales	Gales
Northern Ireland	Irlanda del Norte
Ireland	Irlanda
Spain	España
Portugal	Portugal
France	Francia
Italy	Italia
Germany	Alemania

COUNTRIES

Holland	Holanda
Belgium	Bélgica
Norway	Noruega
Sweden	Suecia
Denmark	Dinamarca
United States	Estados Unidos
Canada	Canadá
Australia	Australia
New Zealand	Nueva Zelanda
Russia	Rusia
China	China
Japan	Japón

COUNTRYSIDE

countryside	campo
landscape	paisaje
nature	naturaleza
view	vista
mountain	montaña
hill	colina
valley	valle
river	río
stream	arroyo
lake	lago
forest	bosque
farm	granja

DAIRY PRODUCTS

dairy products	lácteos
milk	leche
butter	mantequilla
margarine	margarina
cheese	queso
yogurt	yogur
cream	nata
ice cream	helado
milk shake	batido
whole milk	leche entera
skimmed milk	leche desnatada

DAY

day	día
morning	mañana
afternoon	tarde
evening	tarde
night	noche
midday	mediodía
midnight	medianoche
early morning	madrugada
sunrise	salida del sol
sunset	puesta del sol
early	temprano
late	tarde

DELICATESSEN

delicatessen	charcutería
cooked meats	fiambres
ham	jamón
pork loin	lomo
spicy sausage	chorizo
salami	salami
cheese	queso
goat's cheese	queso de cabra
sheep's cheese	queso de oveja
mature cheese	queso curado
olives	aceitunas
olive oil	aceite de oliva

DESSERTS

dessert	postre
ice cream	helado
sorbet	sorbete
apple tart	tarta de manzana
rice pudding	arroz con leche
chocolate mousse	mousse de chocolate
crème caramel	flan
custard dessert	natillas
cheesecake	tarta de queso
cream	nata

DIRECTIONS

right	derecha
left	izquierda
straight on	todo recto
cross	cruce
turn	doble
corner	esquina
roundabout	rotonda
opposite	enfrente
next to	al lado de
behind	detrás de
near	cerca
far	lejos

DRIVING

car	coche
driver	conductor
driving licence	carné de conducir
insurance	seguro
registration	matrícula
car key	llave de coche
seat belt	cinturón
roof rack	baca
child seat	asiento de niño
breakdown	avería
tow truck	grúa
petrol station	gasolinera

DRIVING

petrol	gasolina
unleaded	sin plomo
diesel	diesel / gasóleo
oil	aceite
air	aire
water	agua
road	carretera
dual c/way	autovía
motorway	autopista
toll	peaje
roadworks	obras
diversion	desvío

DRIVING

garage	taller
battery	batería
tyre	neumático
puncture	pinchazo
brakes	frenos
exhaust pipe	tubo de escape
windscreen	parabrisas
indicator	intermitente
lights	luces
door	puerta
bonnet	capó
boot	maletero

FAMILY

family	familia
parents	padres
father	padre
mother	madre
son	hijo
daughter	hija
brother	hermano
sister	hermana
grandfather	abuelo
grandmother	abuela
grandson	nieto
granddaughter	nieta

FAMILY

uncle	tío
aunt	tía
nephew	sobrino
niece	sobrina
cousin	primo
husband	marido
wife	esposa
children	hijos
father-in-law	suegro
mother-in-law	suegra
son-in-law	yerno
daughter-in-law	nuera

FISH

fish	pescado
salmon	salmón
tuna	atún
sardines	sardinas
cod	bacalao
hake	merluza
sole	lenguado
monkfish	rape
red mullet	salmonete
swordfish	pez espada
sea bass	lubina
red bream	besugo

FOOTBALL

football	fútbol
footballer	futbolista
ball	balón
stadium	estadio
pitch	campo
team	equipo
player	jugador
match	partido
referee	árbitro
penalty	penalty
corner	córner
goal	gol

FRUIT

fruit	fruta
apple	manzana
orange	naranja
lemon	limón
pear	pera
banana	plátano
grape	uva
melon	melón
pineapple	piña
strawberry	fresa
peach	melocotón
cherry	cereza

GARDEN

garden	jardín
gardener	jardinero
garden centre	viveros
grass	césped
flowers	flores
tree	árbol
shrub	arbusto
plant	planta
soil	tierra
fence	valla
awning	toldo
barbecue	barbacoa

HAIR

hair	pelo
brush	cepillo
comb	peine
shampoo	champú
conditioner	acondicionador
mousse	espuma
hairspray	laca
hairdresser's	peluquería
cut	corte
style	peinado
dye	tinte
highlights	reflejos

HEALTH

health	salud
illness	enfermedad
pain	dolor
cough	tos
sore throat	dolor de garganta
cold	resfriado
flu	gripe
fever	fiebre
diarrhoea	diarrea
vomiting	vómitos
constipation	estreñimiento

HERBS & SPICES

herb	hierba
parsley	perejil
thyme	tomillo
oregano	orégano
rosemary	romero
basil	albahaca
spice	especia
salt	sal
pepper	pimienta
paprika	pimentón
garlic	ajo
saffron	azafrán

HOSPITAL

hospital	hospital
patient	paciente
appointment	cita
check-up	revisión
doctor	médico
nurse	enfermero
consultant	especialista
ward	sala
waiting room	sala de espera
accident & emergency	urgencias

HOTEL

hotel	hotel
reservation	reserva
reception	recepción
key	llave
bill	cuenta
room	habitación
single room	individual
double room	doble
breakfast	desayuno
half board	media pensión
full board	pensión completa

HOTEL

dining room	comedor
lounge	salón
bar	bar
lift	ascensor
safe	caja fuerte
balcony	balcón
swimming pool	piscina
heating	calefacción
air-conditioning	aire acondicionado
parking	aparcamiento
garage	garaje

HOUSE

house	casa
door	puerta
key	llave
living room	salón
bedroom	dormitorio
bathroom	cuarto de baño
kitchen	cocina
toilet	aseo
utility room	lavadero
balcony	balcón
roof terrace	azotea
garden	jardín

HOUSE

roof	techo
stairs	escalera
window	ventana
blind	persiana
alarm	alarma
water	agua
gas	gas
electricity	electricidad
heating	calefacción
boiler	caldera
air-conditioning	aire acondicionado

HOUSE REPAIR

repair	arreglo
maintenance	mantenimiento
alteration	reforma
builder	albañil
electrician	electricista
plumber	fontanero
carpenter	carpintero
locksmith	cerrajero
glazier	cristalero
painter	pintor
ironmonger's	ferretería
DIY	bricolaje

JEWELLERY

jewellery	joyas
jeweller's	joyería
watch	reloj
ring	anillo
necklace	collar
bracelet	pulsera
brooch	broche
earring	pendiente
chain	cadena
cuff link	gemelo
gold	oro
silver	plata

KITCHEN

kitchen	cocina
oven	horno
hob	placa
fridge	frigorífico
freezer	congelador
washing m/c	lavadora
dishwasher	lavavajillas
microwave	microondas
kettle	hervidor
toaster	tostador
saucepan	cazo
frying pan	sartén

KITCHEN

crockery	vajilla
plate	plato
dinner plate	plato llano
soup dish	plato hondo
cup	taza
saucer	platillo
teapot	tetera
jug	jarra
glass	vaso
wine glass	copa de vino
salad bowl	ensaladera
fruit bowl	frutero

KITCHEN

cutlery	cubiertos
knife	cuchillo
fork	tenedor
spoon	cuchara
teaspoon	cucharilla
soup spoon	cuchara sopera
ladle	cucharón
peeler	pelador
grater	rallador
tin opener	abrelatas
bottle opener	abrebotellas
corkscrew	sacacorchos

LAW

law	ley
lawyer	abogado
contract	contrato
signature	firma
notary	notario
deposit	depósito
witness	testigo
will	testamento
house deeds	escritura
licence	permiso
residence permit	permiso de residencia

LIVING ROOM

living room	salón
sofa	sofá
armchair	sillón
sideboard	aparador
table	mesa
chair	silla
curtains	cortinas
cushion	cojín
rug	alfombra
picture	cuadro
clock	reloj
lamp	lámpara

MEAT

meat	carne
steak	bistec
beef	ternera
lamb	cordero
pork	cerdo
chicken	pollo
turkey	pavo
duck	pato
rabbit	conejo
chop	chuleta
breast	pechuga
sirloin	solomillo

MONTHS

January	enero
February	febrero
March	marzo
April	abril
May	mayo
June	junio
July	julio
August	agosto
September	septiembre
October	octubre
November	noviembre
December	diciembre

NATIONALITIES

nationality	nacionalidad
British	británico
English	inglés
Scottish	escocés
Welsh	galés
Northern Irish	norirlandés
Irish	irlandés
Spanish	español
Portuguese	portugués
French	francés
German	alemán
Italian	italiano

NUMBERS

number	número
zero	cero
one	uno
two	dos
three	tres
four	cuatro
five	cinco
six	seis
seven	siete
eight	ocho
nine	nueve
ten	diez

NUMBERS

eleven	once
twelve	doce
thirteen	trece
fourteen	catorce
fifteen	quince
sixteen	dieciséis
seventeen	diecisiete
eighteen	dieciocho
nineteen	diecinueve
twenty	veinte
twenty-one	veintiuno
twenty-two	veintidós

NUMBERS

thirty	treinta
forty	cuarenta
fifty	cincuenta
sixty	sesenta
seventy	setenta
eighty	ochenta
ninety	noventa
one hundred	cien
two hundred	doscientos
five hundred	quinientos
thousand	mil
million	millón

OPTICIAN'S

optician's	óptica
eye	ojo
eye test	examen de ojos
appointment	cita
glasses	gafas
frame	montura
lens	cristal
contact lens	lentilla
sunglasses	gafas de sol
glasses case	estuche
short-sighted	miope
long-sighted	hipermétrope

PARK

park	parque
gardens	jardines
grass	césped
trees	árboles
flowers	flores
lake	lago
fountain	fuente
statue	estatua
kiosk	kiosco
bench	banco
swings	columpios
slide	tobogán

PEOPLE

people	gente
man	hombre
woman	mujer
boy	niño
girl	niña
children	niños
young person	joven
pensioner	pensionista
friend	amigo
boyfriend	novio
girlfriend	novia
neighbour	vecino

PERSONAL DETAILS

name	nombre
surname	apellido
address	domicilio
postcode	código postal
telephone	teléfono
male	varón
female	mujer
married	casado
single	soltero
age	edad
date of birth	fecha de nacimiento

POLICE

police	policía
police station	comisaría
police officer	agente de policía
accident	accidente
witness	testigo
statement	declaración
offence	delito
fine	multa
theft	robo
legal	legal
illegal	ilegal

POST OFFICE

post office	Correos
postman	cartero
postbox	buzón
letter	carta
envelope	sobre
stamp	sello
address	dirección
postcode	código postal
airmail	por avión
parcel	paquete
fragile	frágil
urgent	urgente

PUBLIC TRANSPORT

airport	aeropuerto
taxi	taxi
bus	autobús
train	tren
underground	metro
timetable	horario
ticket office	taquilla
ticket	billete
single	ida
return	ida y vuelta
platform	andén
left-luggage	consigna

RESTAURANT

restaurant	restaurante
reservation	reserva
waiter	camarero
dining room	comedor
terrace	terraza
lunch	almuerzo
dinner	cena
menu	carta
set menu	menú del día
wine list	carta de vinos
bill	cuenta
toilets	servicios

RESTAURANT

bread	pan
starters	entradas
soup	sopa
salad	ensalada
meat	carnes
fish	pescados
seafood	mariscos
rice dishes	arroces
dessert	postres
still water	agua sin gas
sparkling water	agua con gas

SALAD

salad	ensalada
lettuce	lechuga
tomato	tomate
onion	cebolla
cucumber	pepino
pepper	pimiento
olives	aceitunas
asparagus	espárrago
avocado	aguacate
radish	rábano
beetroot	remolacha
celery	apio

SEAFOOD

seafood	mariscos
prawns	gambas
king prawn	langostino
lobster	langosta
mussels	mejillones
clams	almejas
oyster	ostra
scallops	vieiras
squid	calamares
octopus	pulpo
cuttlefish	sepia
crab	cangrejo

SHOES

shoe shop	zapatería
footwear	calzado
shoe	zapato
boot	bota
trainer	zapatilla de deporte
sandal	sandalia
flip-flop	chancla
slipper	zapatilla
shoe polish	betún
heel	tacón
sole	suela

SHOPPING

shop	tienda
price	precio
size	talla
changing room	probador
till	caja
receipt	recibo
discount	descuento
sale	rebajas
shopping centre	centro comercial
department store	grandes almacenes

SIGHTSEEING

tourist office	oficina de turismo
information	información
town map	plano
places of interest	lugares de interés
timetable	horario
guide book	guía
ticket	entrada
excursion	excursión
souvenir	souvenir
postcard	postal

SIGHTSEEING

main square	plaza mayor
palace	palacio
castle	castillo
cathedral	catedral
church	iglesia
museum	museo
monument	monumento
park	parque
gardens	jardines
stadium	estadio
river	río
view	vista

SIGNS

entrance	entrada
exit	salida
push	empujar
pull	tirar
for sale	se vende
for rent	se alquila
out of order	no funciona
danger	peligro
no smoking	prohibido fumar
no parking	prohibido aparcar

SNACKS

bar snacks	tapas
portion	ración
half portion	media ración
ham	jamón
cheese	queso
prawns	gambas
croquettes	croquetas
meatballs	albóndigas
Spanish omelette	tortilla de patatas
spicy potatoes	patatas bravas
Russian salad	ensaladilla rusa

SOFT DRINKS

soft drink	refresco
juice	zumo
orange	naranja
lemon	limón
pineapple	piña
peach	melocotón
lemonade	gaseosa
ice	hielo
crushed ice drink	granizado
fresh orange juice	zumo de naranja natural

SPIRITS

spirits	licores
whisky	whisky
gin	ginebra
vodka	vodka
rum	ron
brandy	brandy
soda	soda
tonic	tónica
ginger ale	ginger ale
lemonade	gaseosa
water	agua
ice	hielo

STATIONERY

stationer's	papelería
paper	papel
pen	bolígrafo
pencil	lápiz
ink	tinta
envelope	sobre
folder	carpeta
notebook	cuaderno
diary	agenda
photocopy	fotocopia
fax	fax
laminated	plastificado

SUPERMARKET

supermarket	supermercado
meat	carnes
fish	pescados
fruit	frutas
vegetables	verduras
dairy products	lácteos
delicatessen	charcutería
bakery	panadería
frozen food	congelados
tinned food	conservas
drinks	bebidas
wines	vinos

SUPERMARKET

tea	té
coffee	café
milk	leche
sugar	azúcar
bread	pan
butter	mantequilla
margarine	margarina
jam	mermelada
honey	miel
cereals	cereales
juice	zumo
water	agua

SUPERMARKET

eggs	huevos
bacon	bacon
sausage	salchicha
sauce	salsa
ketchup	ketchup
mayonnaise	mahonesa
mustard	mostaza
soup	sopa
rice	arroz
salt	sal
pepper	pimienta
oil	aceite

SUPERMARKET

tissues	pañuelos
nappy	pañal
toilet roll	papel higiénico
kitchen roll	rollo de cocina
detergent	detergente
softener	suavizante
bleach	lejía
polish	cera
batteries	pilas
light bulb	bombilla
washing-up liquid	lavavajillas

TEA & COFFEE

tea	té
milk	leche
sugar	azúcar
herbal tea	infusión
mint tea	menta poleo
camomile tea	manzanilla
coffee	café
white coffee	café con leche
black coffee	café americano
espresso	café solo
cappuccino	capuchino
decaffeinated	descafeinado

TELEPHONE

telephone	teléfono
number	número
call	llamada
message	mensaje
answerphone	contestador
mobile	móvil
top-up	recarga
SIM card	tarjeta SIM
landline	teléfono fijo
phone card	tarjeta telefónica
coin	moneda

TIME

second	segundo
minute	minuto
hour	hora
quarter hour	cuarto de hora
half hour	media hora
day	día
week	semana
weekend	fin de semana
working day	día laborable
fortnight	quincena
month	mes
year	año

TOILETRIES

soap	jabón
shampoo	champú
conditioner	acondicionador
shower gel	gel de ducha
deodorant	desodorante
antiperspirant	antitranspirante
moisturizer	crema hidratante
toothpaste	pasta de dientes
safety razor	maquinilla de afeitar

UTILITY ROOM

utility room	lavadero
mop	fregona
bucket	cubo
cloth	trapo
dustpan	recogedor
brush	cepillo
clothes airer	tendedero
iron	plancha
ironing board	tabla de planchar
washing machine	lavadora

VEGETABLES

vegetables	verduras
potato	patata
carrot	zanahoria
onion	cebolla
cauliflower	coliflor
cabbage	col
peas	guisantes
green beans	judías verdes
spinach	espinaca
broccoli	brócoli
aubergine	berenjena
sweetcorn	maíz dulce

WEATHER

weather	tiempo
forecast	pronóstico
temperature	temperatura
heat	calor
sunny	soleado
hot	caluroso
cold	frío
cool	fresco
cloudy	nuboso
rain	lluvia
wind	viento
storm	tormenta

WINE

wine	vino
red wine	vino tinto
white wine	vino blanco
rosé wine	vino rosado
sparkling wine	cava
champagne	champán
sherry	jerez
port	oporto
sweet	dulce
dry	seco
glass	copa
bottle	botella

YEAR

year	año
spring	primavera
summer	verano
autumn	otoño
winter	invierno
Christmas	Navidad
New Year	Año Nuevo
Christmas Eve	Nochebuena
New Year's Eve	Nochevieja
Easter week	Semana Santa
public holiday	día festivo
holiday	vacaciones

Spanish Pronunciation

Pronunciation

Pronunciation Summary

Spanish Word Stress

Spanish Pronunciation

ce

In Spanish ce is pronounced like the th in thanks.

Practise saying this th sound with these Spanish words:

cerca	near
cero	zero
cerdo	pig
centro	centre
cesta	basket

Spanish Pronunciation

▪ ci

In Spanish ci is pronounced like the th in thanks.

Practise saying this th sound with these Spanish words.

cinco	five
cita	appointment
cien	one hundred
circo	circus
circular	circular

Spanish Pronunciation

▪ e

In Spanish e at the end of a word is pronounced like a – the first letter of the English alphabet.

Practise saying this a sound with these Spanish words.

madre	mother
padre	father
coche	car
leche	milk
grande	big

Spanish Pronunciation

▪ ge

In Spanish ge is pronounced like the ch in the Scottish word loch. This is a back-of-the-throat sound as if clearing the throat!

Practise saying this throaty loch sound with these Spanish words.

general	general
generoso	generous
genial	brilliant
gente	people
gel	gel

Spanish Pronunciation

▪ gi

In Spanish gi is pronounced like the ch in the Scottish word loch. This is a back-of-the-throat sound as if clearing the throat!

Practise saying this throaty loch sound with these Spanish words.

ginebra	gin
gimnasta	gymnast
gimnasio	gym
gitano	gypsy
gira	tour

Spanish Pronunciation

∎ h

In Spanish h has no sound.
It is a silent letter.

Practise saying these Spanish
words making sure h has no
sound.

hola	hello
hora	hour
hoy	today
hombre	man
hospital	hospital

Spanish Pronunciation

▪ j

In Spanish j is pronounced like the ch in the Scottish word loch. This is a back-of-the throat sound as if clearing the throat!

Practise saying this throaty loch sound with these Spanish words.

jamón	ham
jardín	garden
jarra	jug
junio	June
julio	July

Spanish Pronunciation

▪ ll

In Spanish ll is pronounced like the y in yes.

Practise saying this y sound with these Spanish words.

tortilla	omelette
castillo	castle
cuchillo	knife
botella	bottle
caballo	horse

Spanish Pronunciation

■ ñ

In Spanish ñ is pronounced like ny in canyon.

Practise saying this ny sound with these Spanish words.

España	Spain
mañana	tomorrow
montaña	mountain
piña	pineapple
Señorita	Miss

Spanish Pronunciation

■ V

In Spanish v at the beginning of a word is pronounced like b in big.

Practise saying this b sound with these Spanish words.

vino	wine
verano	summer
verde	green
vaso	glass
vale	okay

Spanish Pronunciation

▪ Z

In Spanish z is pronounced like the th in thanks.

Practise saying this th sound with these Spanish words.

zumo	juice
zapato	shoe
zona	area
plaza	square
taza	cup

Spanish Pronunciation

Summary

ce, ci and z is th in thanks

e at the end of a word is a – the sound of the first letter of the English alphabet.

ge, gi and j is ch in loch

h is silent

ll is y in yes

ñ is ny in canyon

v at the start of a word is b in big

Spanish Pronunciation

Word Stress

Spanish words are normally stressed on the last syllable.

actor normal papel popular

But if a Spanish word ends in a, e, i, o, u, s or n the stress is on the last-but-one syllable.

nota arte plato intenso

If a Spanish word has an accent (´) the stress is on the accent.

bebé melón adiós teléfono

SPAIN GUIDE

The Highlights of Spain

Maps of Mainland Spain and the Spanish Islands

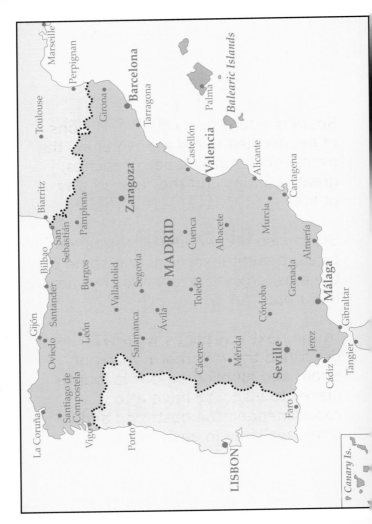

Spain

Spain is a fantastic country. Millions of people visit every year to enjoy the excellent climate, superb beaches, great facilities and the relaxed way of life.

Spain also has wonderful towns and cities, beautiful scenery and some of the most enjoyable festivals anywhere in Europe.

In the next few pages we have described the different regions of Spain and highlighted our favourite places to visit. We have also recommended the best food and drink available in each region.

Southern Spain

Andalucía covers all of southern Spain and runs for over 350 miles from the Portuguese border in the west to the province of Almería in the east. Andalucía is a beautiful and popular region of Spain.

There are excellent beaches all along the coastline. The best beaches are on the Atlantic coast of the Costa de la Luz and along the Mediterranean coast of Almería. Inland there are dramatic mountain ranges and beautiful landscapes.

The cities of Granada, Córdoba and Seville have some of the most interesting and important monuments in Europe and are great places to visit. Andalucía is also famous for some of the most colourful and exciting festivals held in Spain.

Highlights of Southern Spain

Places to Visit

Granada's Alhambra palace and gardens. Córdoba's Mezquita mosque and the old town. Seville's Alcázar palace and gardens, Giralda tower and old town. The attractive towns and cities of Cádiz, Jerez and Ronda.

Food and Drink

chilled soups	gazpacho & salmorejo
fried fish	fritura de pescado
cured ham	jamón ibérico
bar snacks	tapas

draught beer	caña
dry sherry	fino & manzanilla
fruit punch	sangría
red wine & lemonade	tinto de verano

Eastern Spain

Eastern Spain consists of the regions of Cataluña, Valencia and Murcia. This large region stretches for over 500 miles from the French border in the north to Andalucía in the south.

This region has some of the best scenery in Spain. The Costa Brava, the area around Dénia and the Mar Menor are exceptionally beautiful. The east coast is home to some of the best known holiday resorts in Spain attracting millions of visitors because of the excellent climate, great beaches and superb facilities.

Barcelona is the cultural and commercial capital of Cataluña and one of the best cities in Europe. Valencia and Murcia are also important and attractive regional capitals.

Highlights of Eastern Spain

Places to Visit

Barcelona's Sagrada Familia cathedral, Gaudi's buildings and Park Güell, the old town and La Rambla. Valencia's historic centre and City of Arts and Sciences. Alicante's beach, seafront and marina. The attractive centres of Gerona, Murcia, Elche and Cartagena.

Food and Drink

paella & rice dishes	arroces
shellfish & noodles	fideuá
Catalan sausage	butifarra
fresh salad	ensalada
fresh fruit	fruta del tiempo

sparkling wine	cava
white wines	Penedés region
red wines	Priorato region
rosé wines	Ampurdán

Northern Spain

Northern Spain includes the regions of Galicia, Asturias, Cantabria, the Basque Country and Navarra. It runs for 350 miles from the Atlantic in the west to the Pyrenees in the east. This area has a cooler and wetter climate than the rest of the country and is sometimes called "Green Spain".

The coastline of Galicia is especially beautiful and there are excellent beaches all along the north coast. The mountains of the Picos de Europa and the Spanish Pyrenees have some of the best scenery in Spain.

This region hosts the beautiful resorts of San Sebastián and Santander and the attractive cities of Santiago de Compostela, Oviedo and La Coruña. Bilbao is home to the fantastic Guggenheim Museum.

Highlights of Northern Spain

Places to Visit

Santiago de Compostela's **cathedral
and old town.** San Sebastián's **bay,
beaches and headlands.** Santander's
bays and beaches. Oviedo's **old town.**

The stunning coastline of Galicia.

Food and Drink

fresh fish	pescados
seafood	mariscos
tuna pie	empanada de atún
bean stew	fabada asturiana
blue cheese	cabrales
white wines	Albariño, Ribeiro, Rías Baixas
cider	sidra
liqueur	orujo

Central Spain

Central Spain covers a huge area from Andalucía in the south to Asturias and Cantabria in the north, from the Portuguese border in the west to Cataluña, Valencia and Murcia in the east. To the south of Madrid there is Castille La Mancha and Extremadura and to the north Castille and León, La Rioja and Aragón.

This massive plain has incredible blue skies throughout the year and is only broken up by mountain ranges to the north and west of Madrid.

Spain's fantastic capital city is in the centre of this region and almost exactly in the centre of Spain. Around Madrid cities like Salamanca, Segovia, Toledo and Ávila are some of the most historic and beautiful cities in Spain.

Highlights of Central Spain

Places to Visit

Madrid's **Plaza Mayor, Royal Palace and the Thyssen, Prado and Reina Sofía museums. The Retiro Park and gardens.**
León's **cathedral and old town.**
Salamanca's **Plaza Mayor and old town.**
Ávila's **city walls and historic centre.**
Segovia's **Alcázar and aqueduct.**
Toledo's **cathedral, historic centre and El Greco paintings.**

Food and Drink

roast lamb	cordero asado
suckling pig	cochinillo asado
ratatouille	pisto manchego
ham	jamón ibérico
cheese	queso manchego
red wines	Rioja, Ribera del Duero
white wines	Rueda, Rioja

The Spanish Islands

Spain has two groups of islands, the Balearic Islands in the Mediterranean and the Canary Islands off the coast of Morocco in the Atlantic.

The Balearic Islands consist of Mallorca, Menorca, Ibiza and Formentera. The Balearics have stunning coastlines, beautiful coves, excellent beaches and some of the best tourist facilities in Europe. Palma de Mallorca, Ibiza and Mahón are lively and attractive capital cities.

The Canary Islands are Gran Canaria, Lanzarote, Fuerteventura, Tenerife, La Gomera, El Hierro and La Palma. The Canaries have an excellent year round climate, dramatic volcanic landscapes, some excellent beaches and vibrant capital cities in Las Palmas de Gran Canaria and Santa Cruz de Tenerife.

Highlights of the Islands

Places to Visit

Balearics - Palma, Ibiza, Mahón and Ciutadella. The beaches of northern Mallorca, southern Menorca and Ibiza.
Canaries - Las Palmas, Santa Cruz de Tenerife. The beaches of Gran Canaria and Fuerteventura. Volcanic landscapes in Lanzarote and Tenerife.

Food and Drink

Balearics
breakfast pastry	ensaimada
Menorcan cheese	queso de Mahón
local wine	Binissalem

The Canaries
fresh fish	pescados
salted potatoes	papas arrugadas
spicy sauce	mojo colorado
rum	ron

Balearic Islands

Menorca
Ciutadella
Mahón
Mallorca
Alcúdia
Sóller
Palma
Cabrera
Ibiza
Ibiza
San Antonio
Formentera
Castellón de la Plana
Valencia
Dénia

Canary Islands

Lanzarote
Arrecife
Fuerteventura
Puerto del Rosario
Gran Canaria
Las Palmas
Tenerife
Santa Cruz de Tenerife
La Palma
Santa Cruz de La Palma
La Gomera
San Sebastián
El Hierro
Valverde

Index-Índice

Index-Índice